An Introduction to Technical Theatre

Published by Tualatin Books, an imprint of Pacific University Press

2043 College Way
Forest Grove, Oregon 97116

Cover design by Alex Bell

ISBN (pbk) 978-1-945398-87-2
ISBN (epub) 978-1-945398-70-4
ISBN (PDF) 978-1-945398-71-1

Published in the United States of America

First Edition

An Introduction to Technical Theatre

Written and Illustrated by Tal Sanders

TUALATIN
BOOKS

About this Book

I have taught technical theatre classes for many years using some of the major texts on this subject, and while there are some quite comprehensive texts available, I wanted something that could speak more specifically to the needs of my students. I wanted to create a text that covered the basics, including theatre terminology and general practices, but was not so in-depth as to overwhelm those who were studying technical theatre as an elective part of their education. It occurred to me that my situation and students are not unique and that a text of this type might be of use to many.

This text is intended to be a learning resource for classes at both high school and college program levels. It is written in a modular format to help others, like myself, who regularly rearrange their syllabus around productions and space scheduling. Highlighted terms throughout the text indicate important theatrical terminology and are included in the glossary. As the text is modular, some terms may be highlighted in several sections upon first use therein. Boxed information under "There's more to know" or "Consider this" headers provides further information and ideas that relate to the text.

This book has come from my experience in this art form both in and out of the classroom over the last 30+ years. While I have tried to be inclusive and to avoid being overly controversial, I appreciate that there are many schools of thought regarding the intricacies of producing within this art form and expect some instructors may take exception to a term or point of view.

Cost is also a factor for my students. We would like to think the cost of our required textbooks pays off over time as they are continuously used as reference, but I am not sure that logic always applies to the modern student. Offered as an OA text, this book is intended to be free to all interested readers. It is my hope that by eliminating the cost this knowledge will readily spread, helping new students find the passion for this art that I love.

—Tal Sanders

The author wishes to thank:

Aaron Levin, Isaac Gilman, Johanna Meetz, Brent Sullivan, and the fall 2016 Theatre-120 class at Pacific University for their support of this text, and all of the mentors, collaborators, and students who have helped me find my passion for this art.

Theatre: A Collaborative Art

Among the arts, theatre is unique in that at its very core it is **collaborative**. Unlike authoring a book or painting a great masterpiece, a piece of theatre has not come from the mind of a single creator, but from a large group of people working toward a common goal. The theatre collaboration is similar to the function of a sports team, or even a military unit, in that many people are doing a variety of things that all contribute to the group success. This group of artists collaborates to conceive and construct a performance that endeavors to entertain its audiences. Each of the artists involved in this process contributes uniquely to the final product. Some of these contributions are obvious, some are more hidden but no less important to the creative whole.

There is an art, or at least a skill, to successful collaboration. Many of you have participated in group activities and team sports and can identify with both the power of group (team) work and the common struggles within groups to adopt a single vision. These factors exemplify both the challenge and the strength of theatre collaborations.

When working within a group, we must navigate differences of opinion, entertain varying perspectives, and rise to the challenge of maintaining clear communication. Learning to listen is an important skill in this scenario. Being clear in thought, exact in language, and deliberate in choice of illustrative examples can be key to success.

Theatre artists must learn the difference between giving up on our ideas when a strong voice is advocating for something different and defending our views to the point that we become an obstacle to consensus. I have found when artists listen closely and truly attempt to understand one another they are often able to find solutions that incorporate and even enhance seemingly disparate ideas.

In theatre we must channel our ideas in support of the direction in which the entire production is moving. Falling silent when you have a solution or shutting down when your ideas cannot be incorporated does a disservice to the entire production. A skilled collaborator will find an appropriate opportunity and use a productive tone to offer their opinions.

For many of us, our sense of how a theatrical production is put together stems from our experiences with theatre in our schools. For example, many students have participated in a drama program at their high school. These experiences may lead us to the conclusion that all productions are created under a system wherein the show's **director** makes virtually every decision and everyone else involved is trying their best to carry out the director's plan. It is easy to understand why we might have that impression when many of our schools have theatre programs in which the director is the only permanent staff and designers and other specialists are only brought in when required or when their talents can be afforded.

Many small community theatres and even college theatres, may, due to their limited staffing for productions, leave us with a similar impression that top-down management is the only style used in theatres. However, the way most **professional** theatre companies produce their shows constitutes more of a shared-responsibility model. In these companies, an entire team works together toward a cohesive solution that incorporates everyone's expertise.

This is not to say the director's influence on the production is diminished or that they do not carry an overarching responsibility for all elements of the production, but more that they are usually surrounded by other artists working on the production who bring their own experience and imagination to ensure it can be realized to its fullest extent. A director's job includes unifying the artistic vision of the entire **company**. When looking at the reporting structure for most theatre organizations you see designers and other production staff do maintain a reporting relationship to the director.

An inclusive spirit is at the center of a productive and successful collaboration. When carried through all levels of production and performance—from the producers and director to the stage manager and technicians—these individuals work together, bringing their best so the end product will be a piece of art worthy of their collective investment.

Those who have participated in theatrical productions understand this environment fosters a special camaraderie among the cast and crew of a show and the experience of being part of a production often feels like having joined a new "family."

Smaller theatre companies and educational theatre programs have a comparatively small staff doing multiple jobs. Much like the high school director mentioned earlier, in these situations a few individuals may wear multiple "hats" required to fulfil the roles in the production.

In a typical professional theatre organization, each individual would hold only one job listed on the company's organizational chart. It is important to think of these models as upward trending lines of artistic responsibility rather than a downward trending workflow chart.

As you can imagine, in many smaller organizations the duties of all thirty job categories listed here must be fulfilled by just a few people. A scaled down organization such as a **community theatre** or educational theatre program might have an organizational chart that is simpler.

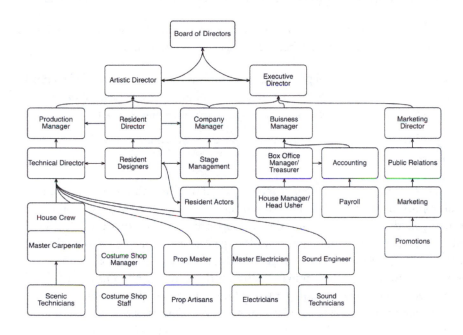

Example of a professional theatre organization model

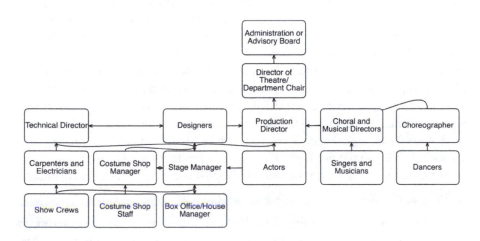

An educational or community theatre organization model

Although all of the duties are still covered here, you can see a relatively small number of people make up the organization's creative staff. Notice the show's director is not at the top of the chart, but rather maintains a reporting relationship to those above. In educational theatre, the show's director may report to the department chair, director of theatre, or even a school principal. In a community theatre, the director may report to and artistically satisfy an artistic director or a board of directors.

Job titles and duties are covered in **Module 2**, but it may be useful now to illustrate a typical scenario of how this theatrical collaboration functions:

A theatre company, school program, or community theatre has decided to produce a play or a season of plays. Each company will have its own reasons for producing the play(s) it choses, as well as for its desire to produce play(s) at all.

There's More to Know

How are plays selected for production? A school program might choose plays based on educational opportunities, topical stories, or strong roles that provide growth opportunities for acting students. A community theatre may produce plays that provide lots of opportunities for involvement and tend towards large cast shows. A professional theatre may consider a group of plays that fits together as a season, peaks public interest, and has good potential to sell tickets. Original theatre productions are often mounted based on the reputation of the playwright. Regardless of the criteria for choices, the people responsible for programming read many plays in order to choose appropriate material for production.

Often plays are chosen with a specific director in mind. The director may have a particular style or resume of experience that makes them a good match for both the script and audience. They may have a great track record of working with a particular theatre group. Whatever the criteria for selection of the director may be, once selected, they are often asked to help form the rest of the **creative team** for the production. This team includes the producer, director, designers, choreographers, and musical directors. Some companies utilize **resident designers** who, as employees of the company, are assigned to a particular production based on their talents and experience. In other productions the director may be asked if they prefer to work with a particular designer or other creative team member and, possibly, if they have preference for a particular stage manager. Once assembled, this team develops an artistic approach to the production known as a **production concept.** This concept expresses the unifying vision that each individual strives to support in creating the production elements.

The production concept is arrived at through careful consideration of the **script**, the reason to produce a specific story for a specific audience, the **production resources**, and the inspiration and insights of the particular creative team.

Consider This

If you are asked to play a part in a production either on stage or behind the scenes, consider the commitment you are making. It will consume more than just your time. You are agreeing to be part of the collaboration and will have to do your very best at your task to uphold the commitment to the entire production.

Once the creative team has agreed on a production concept, each designer develops their portion of the staging design through a series of meetings and discussions. Meeting both as a group and individually, but always in conversation with the director (who is tasked with carrying the concept forward through rehearsals), the creative team then begins to interact with an entire **production team**. Designs are delivered according to scheduled deadlines, and a process of budgeting funds and other resources commences. Actors are **audition**ed, and **cast** and rehearsals begin: **Sets** and **costume**s are constructed; music, projections, and lighting are created; and the entire production team is engaged in the movement toward opening night.

At this point, the creative team is busy supervising and revising their creative work to ensure a cohesive production. Usually, the designers on this team are working an opposite schedule from those directly involved in rehearsals. Designers work closely with the technical director, costume shop manager, or master electrician as their designs are being realized, attending acting rehearsals only occasionally.

There's More to Know

Three types of technical rehearsals are common to most theatres.

A **dry tech** might be the first of these rehearsals. At a dry tech no performers are present, and time is allowed for crews to become familiar with the show elements and rehearse cues and shifts.

The second rehearsal is often a **wet tech**. It includes performers and allows everyone to learn the traffic patterns imperative to the timing of cues and shifts.

A director may also call for a **cue-to-cue** technical rehearsal, where both crew and cast work together on shifts and cues but dialogue in between these actions is not performed in order to allow for more technical rehearsal in a shorter amount of time.

All show elements must be adequately rehearsed and finessed. During these rehearsals, remember to be present, attentive, quiet, and prepared to both jump forward and go back to repeat actions in order to perfect cue timing.

Still, good theatre professionals realize the most important element of collaboration is how the creative work relates to what happens in the **rehearsal room**. This collaboration is where the production comes alive—where the rubber meets the road, where concept meets reality, and inspiration is tempered by practicality. It is where new ideas born from the rehearsal process can inspire opportunities.

The collaborative process continues, now including performers, choreographers, musicians, stage management, and the director—all bringing their own creative energy to the production—throughout the rehearsal process, into the **technical rehearsals**, and all the way to opening night. During this time, the stage manager maintains daily communication to the entire production team, reporting what happens in the rehearsal room. The director continues to meet with the creative team both as a group for **production meetings** and individually with designers and production personnel in order to keep all efforts moving in support of the developing production.

Once construction of the elements is completed, whether built off-site and **loaded in** or built onstage, the next step in the rehearsal process can begin: technical rehearsals. Technical rehearsals occur when all of the various elements of the final production are brought together and can be integrated into a single piece of art ready for an audience. It is during these rehearsals that the elements of sets, lights, projections, costumes, props, music, sound effects, and atmospheric effects are added. This is also when a whole new group of collaborators join the production: the **stage crew**.

During technical rehearsals the creative team is busy refining the production elements into a whole. They work with the director to shape an experience for the audience. Meanwhile, the stage crew works under the direction of the stage manager, rehearsing **scene shifts** and **cues** so that timing of these is both precise and repeatable. These rehearsals can be difficult and taxing as so many elements and people need to be coordinated. Many theatres conduct the bulk of the technical rehearsals over a weekend or two-day period. Often these days are run as ten-out-of-twelve days, meaning that ten hours of the required twelve-hour day are worked in rehearsal. I have heard people describe the technical rehearsal process as similar to "watching paint dry." It is true these rehearsals can seem long and boring if the sequence or cue being worked on doesn't involve you. If the cue does involve you, you may be asked to repeat the same movement or cue multiple times as the coordination is developed. All the efforts of these rehearsals are rewarded when the technical elements and the actions of the actors are seamlessly married into an effective presentation.

After the initial technical rehearsals, dress rehearsals incorporating wardrobe and costume changes begin, followed by **preview performances**, and, finally, opening night followed by the performance run. Up to opening night, the director and the creative team continue to work toward the best production possible within the given circumstances and time available. Most creative team members move on to their next production once a play opens and their services have been rendered. Even the director's work is now complete, and the stage manager takes on the responsibility of delivering a consistent show that preserves the director's vision throughout the production's run.

For many productions, this entire process takes about 8-12 weeks, though it may be longer for a new or complex production. Generally the rehearsal process takes about 4-6 weeks of that time, and performance runs take approximately 1-3 weeks. The rest of the time is typically spent in **preproduction**.

For Further Exploration

Schumacher, Thomas. 2008. *How Does the Show Go On: An Introduction to the Theater*. New York, N.Y: Disney Editions.

Behind the Emerald Curtain: http://www.emeraldcurtain.com/

Organizational Structures

The task of theatrical production requires many specific skills. These skills may be found in a few individuals or delivered by some highly and specifically trained artists and artisans. The collaborative nature of the art of theatre coupled with the need to produce on a specific timeline makes it necessary for theatre organizations to maintain and follow an organizational and communication structure. This Module breaks down that structure, reporting order, and typical duties. Every organization has its own particular distinctions between job titles, duties, and reporting structures, but the descriptions below are fairly standard in the theatre industry.

There's More to Know

People are often struck by the number of jobs it takes to operate a theatre successfully. This list of job titles might have any number of employees working under them depending on the size of the producing organization. Many people who work in the arts are not directly involved in the on-stage work of a stage production, but rather work in support areas that may include audience services, finance, educational outreach, play development, and many others. A number of people have worked their way into production through other related jobs in support areas of theatre companies.

Administration

Board of Directors: Steers and guides the organization. Provides funding and leadership.

Producer (commercial theatre): Secures the performance rights to stage a production, hires the artistic staff, secures the performance space, and provides financial backing for the production.

Artistic Director/Head of Theatre: Provides artistic guidance, chooses the plays that will be performed during the season, hires production directors, and is responsible for the artistic vision and direction of the theatre or organization. Reports to board of directors.

Executive Director / Managing Director: Responsible for the operation and development of the organization. Oversees the day-to-day operations of the theatre including outreach or educational programs, finances, and community relations. Reports to the board of directors.

Production Management

Production Manager: Responsible for the overall technical operation of a theatre company and maintains season budgets and resource allocations. Supervises all technical staff. Reports to the artistic director and executive director.

Technical Director: Responsible for the oversight of technical operations of a theatre, including scenery, lighting, sound, projections, and construction. Works with designers to ensure requirements are achievable, safe, and within budget parameters. Supervises scene shop staff. Dual reporting relationship with both the artistic director and production manager or managing director.

Master Carpenter: Oversees scene shop and show build.

Carpenters: Construct scenery.

Costume Shop Manager: Responsible for the day-to-day operation of the costume facilities. Supervises costume shop workers. Reports to the technical director or production manager.

First Hand: Assists the costume shop manager in day-to-day operations and builds costumes.

Cutter: Cuts fabrics, plans patterns, and builds costumes.

Draper: Drapes garments and builds costumes.

Stitcher: Builds costumes.

Master Electrician: Responsible for the day-to-day operations of the electrical department. Supervises electricians. Reports to the technical director or production manager.

Electricians: Hang, focus, and maintain lighting equipment.

Prop Master: Responsible for the construction or acquisition of all show props. Works with prop designer, scenic designer, stage manager and performers. Reports to director and production manager.

Prop workers / carpenters: Build and maintain show props.

Scenic Artist: Responsible for all painted scenic finishes. Works with scenic designer and technical director. Supervises painters.

Creative

Playwright: Creates and develops the play script. On an original production, may assist the director in interpreting the work and may supply rewrites of script elements.

Production Director: Sets a vision for and brings together the many complex aspects of a theatrical production, including the script, performers, design, and music into a unified production. Reports to the artistic director and executive director.

Assistant Director: Facilitates the director's work on a production. This may include research, blocking notation, taking notes, and working with an ensemble or chorus. Reports to the director.

Musical Director: Responsible for the arrangement and reproduction of live music for a production. Reports to the production director.

Choreographer: Responsible for creating the style and form of dance and movement routines in a production. Works under the production director.

Fight Choreographer: Responsible for creating safe and repeatable action and fight sequences. Works under the production director.

Scenic Designer: Responsible for the development and design of all scenic elements of a production. Reports to the production director and production manager.

Costume Designer: Responsible for the design of all costume elements for a production. Works with the costume shop manager. Reports to the production director and production manager.

Lighting Designer: Responsible for the design and cueing of lighting for a production. Works with the master electrician. Reports to the production director and production manager.

Sound Designer: Responsible for all audio production elements. Reports to the production director and production manager.

Projections Designer: Responsible for all projected elements of a production. Reports to the production director and production manager.

Prop Designer: Responsible for the design of all properties for a production. Works in concert with the scenic designer. Reports to the production director and production manager.

Show Management

Production Stage Manager: Supervises all stage management activities including management personnel and interns. Maintains master schedules for the company. Reports to the production manager.

Stage Manager: Provides practical and organizational support for a production team, including the director, designers, actors, and technicians. Facilitates productive rehearsals, runs technical rehearsals, and represents the director's vision throughout a production's run. Reports to the production director and production manager.

Assistant Stage Manager: Provides production support to the stage manager. Reports to the stage manager.

Crew

Wardrobe Crew: Responsible for the preparation and maintenance of production wardrobe. Work with costume shop manager. Ultimately report to the technical director. Directly report to stage manager during production run.

Shift Crew: Responsible for the movement and daily maintenance for show scenery. Work with scenic designer. Ultimately report to technical director. Directly report to stage manager during production run.

Props Crew: Responsible for setup, storage, and maintenance of prop elements for a production. Work with prop designer and scenic designer. Ultimately report to technical director. Directly report to stage manager during production run.

Dressers: Responsible for setup and assistance of costume dressing and quick changes for performers. Work with wardrobe crew, costume designer, and performers. Ultimately report to technical director. Directly report to stage manager during production run.

Board Operators: Responsible for the running of cues during performances via lighting, sound, and video consoles. Work with designers. Ultimately report to technical director. Directly report to stage manager during production run.

Follow-Spot Operators: Operate moveable spotlights during a production. Work with lighting designer and master electrician. Ultimately report to technical director. Directly report to stage manager during production run.

For Further Exploration

Volz, Jim. 2011. *Working in American Theatre: A Brief History, Career Guide and Resource Book for over 1000 Theatres.* New York: Bloomsbury Methuen Drama.

Production Scheduling

Theatre production is a time-based art form. That is to say, once we set out to produce a play and have set a date for opening night, the race is on! So much must be researched, debated, decided, coordinated, and realized prior to that opening date. If you choose a life in the theatre, you may find the time commitment that ramps up to opening night and then ends sharply upon closing has a great influence on your life outside of the theatre as well. Artists must be very aware of any overlap of production schedules as the process, especially just before a show's opening, can seem all-consuming.

Consider This

Technical directors have been known to view the considerations of production as a triangle whose three sides represent time, funding, and resources. All sides being equal, makes for a strong triangle, but if you cut any of these lengths down, your new shape no longer resembles a strong triangle. It will then be necessary to recoup what has been lost to bring the form back into shape.

Time is an important element in production, although it is not the only factor that must be considered. Your timeline must allow for not only all that must be ready for the production on opening night, but elements required for rehearsal and the juggling of schedules of various departments that might be involved together in specific elements, such as building, painting, and wiring. **Lead time** for specialty materials that need to be ordered may also be included in the timeline.

Funding seems an obvious element because you need to know what the budget is to know how much you can spend. But budget is also directly allied with time. For example, if there is less time than expected to construct elements or if a load-in to the theatre must be accomplished in a shorter period of time than was planned for or ideal, then clearly labor costs will need to increase to make up the difference. The allocation of funds is also dependent, at least in part, on the resources available for the production. If you are working in a community theatre where they maintain a large inventory of props, costumes, and scenic elements, you may be able to **pull** items from stock rather than creating everything from scratch. Likewise, if you do not have a highly talented scenic artist on staff and your design requires intricate painting, then you might have to budget more money to pay a specialist. People and their skills are a very important resource to consider. Labor and materials consume the bulk of funding reserved for production, and labor costs often make up 50-60% of those funds.

Resources also include things such as the theatre space in which you will be performing. Many small companies rent a theatre to perform their works. These companies must consider and minimize the amount of time they occupy the rental facility in order to maximize their budgets. Careful preplanning of the use of time in the space can help immensely in these situations.

When considering a rental space for a production, the presence or absence of all resources, like lighting and sound equipment, should be considered since they can be expensive to rent. Ideally, some of your production design team will be able to tour the space in person before working on their designs. You should always ask for copies of any scaled plans or other technical specifications that are available.

Your checklist might include:

- Does the space have a **lighting control system?** What type and capability?
- Does the space have a **sound system?** What type and capability?
- Does the space provide back stage communication via **headsets**?
- Is there a **stage monitor** in the dressing room areas?
- Is there a **load-in door** or **loading dock**?
- What is the size of the smallest opening (door etc.) that items must load-in through?
- How many patrons does the space seat (i.e. how many tickets can I sell)?
- Does it provide disability access/accommodations?
- How is the sound quality in the space? Is there echo, hollow sounding, or sound leaks from surrounding areas?
- What size is the stage (including playing area and wing space)?
- How many performers can the dressing rooms accommodate? How secure is this area?
- What style electrical **connectors** does the lighting system require? Will adaptor cables be required?
- What types of **playback** media or formats does the sound system support?

Remember, anything the venue does not provide will need to be brought in and set up for a performance, which will add to the budget in rentals, materials, labor, and time.

Time, funding, and resources are all considered in putting together a **production schedule**. Typically, a master production schedule for a season of productions is developed by a team of people, including the artistic director, managing director, company manager, and technical director. The technical director further develops a **build schedule** for each individual production to ensure productions are realized on time and within budget.

Shops base their schedules on dates of completion for each item as well as on a concept of "lead time." Lead time refers to the amount of time necessary for completion and can be broken down into phases to reach that end. A technical director may break down each individual piece required in a show design in order to consider all the phases the piece must go through and the scheduling requirements of each of those phases onto a large spreadsheet. The painters need to begin their work around the same time as the carpenters begin construction, so unless something from stock is available for painting, the first items to be built may need to include things that require the attention of the painters. Careful coordination of both deadlines and workflow are crucial to a successful build schedule.

When companies produce multiple shows, their production schedule must carefully consider use of space for each production. Overlapping productions can put a strain on limited rehearsal and shop spaces, as well as on personnel fulfilling multiple responsibilities. The production stage manager oversees the schedule and use of rehearsal spaces and support services for those spaces during the season.

For Further Exploration

Shanda, Mark, and Dennis Dorn. 2015. *Technical Management for the Performing Arts: Utilizing Time, Talent, and Money*. New York: Routledge.

Theatre Ontario. 2005. "Guide to Producing in Community Theatre." Accessed August 16, 2018. https://www.theatreontario.org/media/9609/publication_guidetoproducing.pdf.

Theatre Spaces

Western European theatre spaces have been evolving since the early days of Greek theatre. Built into hillsides and taking advantage of natural canyons, early Greek theatres allowed for many patrons to comfortably see and hear the presentations, a primary function of all theatre spaces. The Roman theatre adapted the Greek spaces and added features including a large ornate backing wall (skene) and a framing structure adapted from the Greek *proskene* that has evolved into our modern **proscenium arch**. The Renaissance period brought theatre indoors by adding roofs to some auditoriums and developed a heavy reliance on elaborate scenery. A variety of styles of performance spaces have been developed since that time, each with its own achievements in creating comfortable and flexible spaces that nurture a strong relationship between the performers and the audience

Proscenium theatre

The most familiar type of performance space is the proscenium style theatre. It is essentially two rooms: the auditorium holding the audience, and the stage where the performance takes place. A wall joins these two rooms with a picture frame opening allowing the audience to see into the stage. This picture frame opening is the proscenium arch and is often elaborately decorated. The strength of the proscenium arch is that it focuses the audience's attention on the performance area and blocks the audience from seeing backstage areas so the "magic" of the presentation can be preserved.

Proscenium style theatres often allow for the greatest audience capacity; large auditoriums with multiple balconies are possible with this configuration. The potential downside to this type of space is there is a physical and aesthetic boundary created by the proscenium arch. Physically, the performers framed by the arch are at a distance from the audience, which forces their actions to be enlarged so audience members who are further away can read them. The audience may also feel an aesthetic distancing in that the performances seem less immediate as they are happening to someone "in the next room."

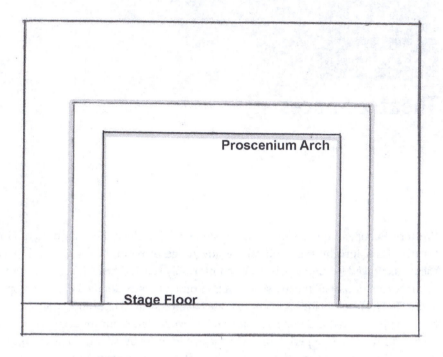

Proscenium theatre front elevation

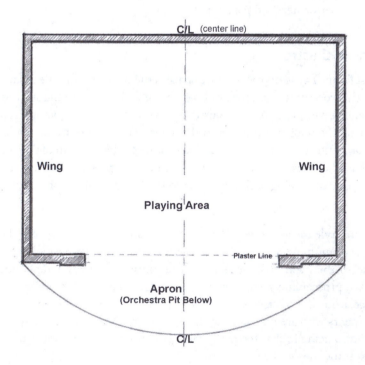

Ground plan

Thrust theatre

Thrust theatre spaces were developed to decrease the distance between audiences and performers, thereby giving the drama a greater sense of intimacy. In a thrust theatre, the apron area has been thrust into the auditorium so the audience surrounds three sides of the playing area. The **upstage** wall remains for scenic representation and entrances and exits. Thrust theatre spaces allow the performers to be quite close to the audiences, but also cause the actors to be very aware of how they must move to be seen by all. In a thrust space, it is an interesting experience for an audience to be looking at other sections of audience as a background to the play. Designers working in these thrust or "three-quarter style" theatres must keep the playing area visible to all by using small or low level objects to transform the stage.

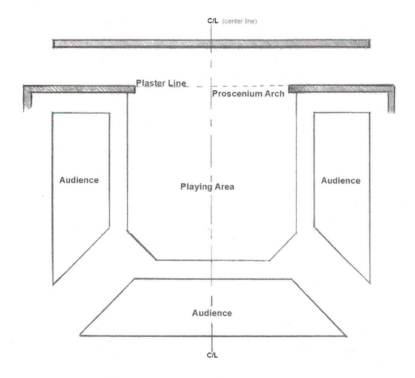

Thrust theatre plan view

Arena theatre

The arena theatre is another format designed for greater intimacy between audiences and performers because it includes seating that completely surrounds the stage. Often circular stages with tiered audiences creating a bowl, these spaces can be scaled from relatively small to arenas seating thousands. Again, like in a thrust environment, acting on an arena stage, or "in the round," requires special attention to "keeping open" so you are always engaging the entire audience surrounding you. The set design must keep from blocking the audience's view, so elaborate scenery in this style auditorium is rare. Instead, designers often rely on small furniture elements and floor coverings to establish scenic locations.

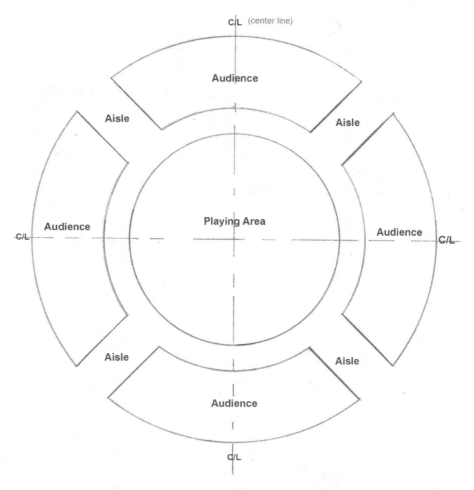

Arena theatre plan view

Black box theatre

The black box theatre is aptly named. These spaces are single rooms that house both the actors and audience. The black box is a flexible space; most have audience seating that is configurable so the room can be adapted for any production. Seating may be set up as "end stage" similar to a proscenium style, on two sides in an "L" configuration, on two opposing sides as a "traverse" layout, or in a three-quarter or arena configuration. Typically, a smaller scaled space, the black box often provides the closest connection between audience and performers. Scenic design for a black box space is largely dependent on the seating arrangement, but in general the intimacy of the space provides less opportunity to hide the "magic" behind the presentation.

Site-specific theatre/found spaces

Site-specific or "found space" performances are held in a variety of locations. If you find a location that supports your story, such as performing in an historic ruin or on an ancient battlefield, you are doing site-specific work. The challenges for these locations may be the lack of traditional support spaces such as dressing rooms for performers, lack of technological resources, and the need to provide audience seating and accommodations. Many companies successfully produce outdoor seasons of classic plays such as Shakespeare in public parks, which could be considered site-specific events.

Found spaces tend to be theatre performance spaces adapted from a room's former use. Warehouses, banks, storefronts, and churches are often converted into found spaces.

For Further Exploration

Brockett, Oscar G., and Franklin J. Hildy. 2006. *History of the Theatre, Foundation Edition.* Boston: Pearson.

History of Theatre. n.d. Accessed August 16, 2018. http://www.historyworld.net/wrldhis/PlainTextHistories.asp?historyid=ab35.

MODULE 5

Our Stages and Their Equipment

Like all other art forms, theatre has developed its own specific terminology to describe its elements of stage craft and equipment. Many of these terms have been handed down through history. Some come to us from the earliest Greek theatres, others from Roman theatre, Renaissance theatre, and other theatre cultures from around the globe. In theatre, it is common for several different terms to be used to describe the same element, and each of these terms is generally deemed to be accurate and acceptable. For the student, this makes the vocabulary of theatre a bit of a challenge to absorb. It also means we should always strive to be specific and consistent in our use of terminology to ensure clear communication.

Consider This

Why is it important to sound like an expert? When working on a show, we rely on one another's expertise to ensure the production is the best it can be. Choosing a collaborator means measuring the success of the project against that team member's skill and their level of commitment. We all want to work with the most talented, dedicated artists, but also with people we can relate to and trust. Trust is always easier to establish with someone who speaks and acts like an expert in the field. Using correct terminology and demonstrating seriousness about your art will always help others instil trust in your ability.

The most confusing terminology in common use for the theatre involves **stage directions**. In order for a production team to be able to reference what part of a stage they are discussing or for a director to talk to a performer about where they should be appearing on the stage, we need to have a set of coordinates to guide us. We refer to these as stage directions. For most, the tricky part is that they are from the perspective of the actor facing the audience. The major areas are downstage (left, right, and center), which is the edge of the stage closest to the audience; mid-stage (left, right, and center); and upstage (left, right, and center) which refers to the area furthest away from the audience. In larger theatres these major areas may be further divided to include a "left of center" and "right of center" as well. We are often in the audience facing the stage when we refer to these coordinates and must remember to reverse our natural sense of direction. During early rehearsals stage managers note all of the actors stage movements, referred to as **blocking,** using this system of coordinates. This blocking is recorded into the script of stage manager's **prompt book** for production reference. Conversely, we also use the terms "**house** right" and "house left" when referring to the seating area of the auditorium as we face the stage. In arena theatres these directions are impractical, and many companies instead use a clock-face model to divide the playing area.

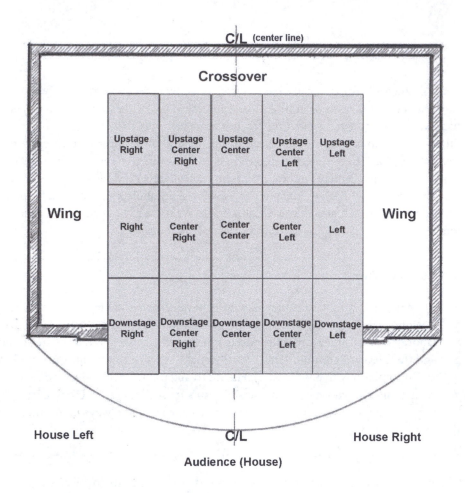

Stage directions

Of the terms we use to describe basic elements of a playing space, some relate most clearly to a proscenium style theatre, but can also be applied to other types of spaces. The area of the stage where the actor is visible to the audience is known as the **playing area**. Space outside the playing area where the audience's view is blocked by scenery, curtains, or the proscenium arch is referred to as **wing** space and can be found both off-stage-left and off-stage-right of the playing area. In a proscenium theatre the area in front of the proscenium arch is referred to as the **apron**.

In some spaces, all or part of this apron may be converted into an **orchestra pit** to house musicians for productions. Some theatres have a **crossover**—a hallway upstage of the playing area or in a basement below the stage that allows for passage from one side of the stage to the other unseen by the audience.

A stage is occasionally equipped with removable panels to create an opening in the floor with access to a basement area. Handy for quick (dis)appearances, these are known as **traps**.

A **control booth** or group of booths is usually found at the rear of the auditorium. This location allows the stage manager and lighting and sound operators to have the same perspective as the audience. Additional booths may be available for followspot operators or other technical needs. In some productions, you see sound operators at a live sound-mixing console in the seating area of the auditorium. This is done so they are able to hear the performance as the audience does rather than from the remote location of a booth or from behind a glass window.

Rigging

Above the stage, you commonly find a **fly system** or theatrical **rigging**. In a proscenium theatre the space above the stage is blocked from the audience's view by the top of the proscenium arch. Depending on how high the ceiling is over the stage, you may be able to **fly** in rigged scenery to transform the stage setting. The area above the stage is referred to as the **fly loft**. At the top of the fly loft is a series of support structures known as the **grid**. From this grid structure a series of cables, pulleys, and ropes supports and moves the hanging elements. If the fly loft is twice as tall as the proscenium, then elements sized to fill the stage can be hidden above for later use. The draperies, scenery, lighting, and other production resources are rigged from this structure via ropes and cables. Modern theatres may be equipped with a **counterweight system** allowing for easier operation and movement of heavy rigged elements. When this is the case, a fly crew can move multiple drops or flying elements via locking control lines running along one wall of the **stage house**. This allows for large scenic transformations with minimal effort. Older theatres may be equipped with **rope-set rigging** where **sandbags** and **tie-off cleats** or a **pin rail** keep the flying elements under control. Most of these theatres place the pin rail about a story above the stage along one wall. This system allows for the flying of production elements as does the counterweight rigging system, although ropes must be carefully tied of by hand rather than simply locked in place.

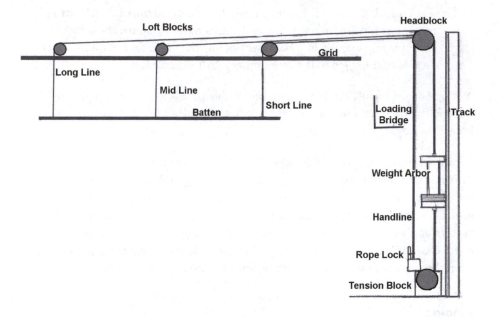

A counterweight arbor system, front view

In both of these rigging systems the support or **lift lines** (whether rope or steel cable) are referred to by their length extending out from the **head block** as short, mid, and long lines. Some wider stage fly systems may require additional spaced lift lines. For rigging, a pulley (or sheave) is housed within in a block, aptly called a **pulley block**. Its job is to change the direction of the rope or line. Several pulleys can be housed in a single block to accommodate multiple lift lines. The pulley blocks directly above the short, mid, and long lines are referred to as **loft blocks** and are supported by the grid. In a rope-set system these lift lines run across the fly loft, through the head block, and down to the pin rail where they can be controlled. Heavy objects are balanced for lifting through the attachment of sandbags. In a counterweight system the lift lines are routed through the head block and then attached to a **counterweight arbor**, which is tracked to run vertically up and down the off-stage wall. This arbor is then loaded with weights using a loading bridge above the stage to counter the load rigged onto a **batten**, which is the horizontal pipe that the lift lines support, and to which scenery, lights, or drapery is rigged. The vertical travel of the arbor is then controlled by the fly crew through the use of a hand-line, which can be locked at any height via the rope lock. The hand-line (or purchase line) is attached to the arbor at the top and bottom. This line runs through the head block at the grid and under the tension block at the stage level. Some battens are capable of supporting the extra weight loads of lighting equipment. These are designated as **electrics** and may also be equipped with permanent electrical circuits for lighting control.

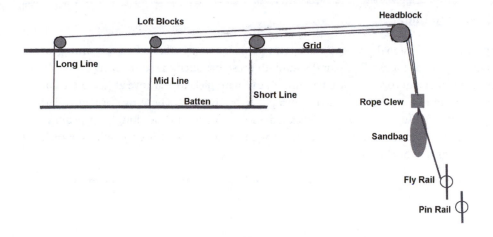

A rope set system (front view)

Consider This

Though the art of rigging has been a part of theatre for centuries, the kind of theatrical spectacles being created today require a special degree of safety oversight. We routinely lift extremely heavy objects above stages and must rely on careful engineering to keep our environments safe. Theatrical rigging standards have been developed for production, and experts should always be consulted when rigging safety is in question.

Fly systems are designed to balance a heavy load hung from a batten so a single individual can move it without great effort. To "fly in" a batten is to bring it down toward the stage floor to be worked on. Conversely a batten is "lifted out." It is customary to always announce to others working around you that a batten or "pipe" is "moving" when you are about to shift its position. This lets everyone know to be on alert for a changing environment and things may be coming in from above. If you are working with a fly system, you should always keep the load-in balance whenever possible to avoid run away lines and keep areas clear when work is being done above.

Sometimes simply balancing a load is not enough for our purposes, and we must gain an advantage over the load for an individual to lift it. That is when we must employ a system of rope and pulleys to aid in lifting the load. You may be familiar with the power of a block and fall set from images of safes or pianos being hauled up into the windows of tall buildings. A block and fall set uses several blocks of pulleys to half the force of the weight of the load we need to haul, but does so by making us move twice the rope through the blocks. Adding more sets of pulleys to the system continues to reduce the force required to lift the load, but also increases the length of rope that must travel through the system.

There's More to Know

On large-scale professional productions cue sequences must be linked to the timing of scene shifts, flying elements, lights, and sound. In these productions some parts of the fly system operation is motorized so that a number of flying pieces can move at just the right speed and in the right order without requiring a large fly crew. These motor-controlled cue sequences are often run by software called Show Control. In addition, large productions often use individual power winches to hang props in the air above the wings, which leaves the wings free of clutter.

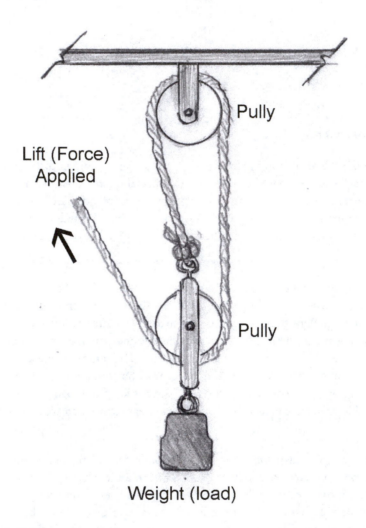

Mechanical Advantage, 2 to 1

Mechanical advantage allows for the use of pulleys to share the weight of a lift line allowing a single technician to lift more than their own weight.

While stage scenery is designed to provide a representation or illusion of the desired location(s) for the play, it is often as important to hide what you *don't* want the audience to see as it is to represent what you *do* want them to take in visually. Rigged from the fly system, theatre draperies create a void that surrounds the performance area.

These drapes help designers to **mask** what they don't want seen. There are specific names for each piece of theatrical drape. The **main drape** or **grand drape** is often richly colored and sits just behind the proscenium arch. This drape traditionally opened to reveal the set at the **top of a show**. It is now common for the set to be exposed when the audience enters the theatre, and so you may only occasionally see this drape closed, but even when open, it is often visible at the edges of the proscenium. Above the main drape is usually a **grand valence** or **grand teaser**. This drape is also richly colored to match the main drape and helps to block the audience's view of the lights and other equipment hanging above in the fly loft. A series of tall but narrow black draperies mask the view into the wing space along both sides of the playing area. These vertical drapes are known as **legs** and **tormentors**. The first set of drapes upstage of the proscenium are termed tormentors and are typically flat-faced, black drapes. The vertical drapes upstage of the tormentors are the legs, which are often pleated. A flat-faced drape known as a **teaser** is a short wide drape hung in front of the set of tormentors to mask the fly gallery equipment. This masking continues upstage with **borders** hung in front of each set of legs. In some theatres, additional masking is hung in the wings running perpendicular to the main drape. These are referred to as **tab** drapes. Theatres may be equipped with a **blackout drape**, a full, stage-width, black drape, or a **blackout traveler** that can be traversed open as needed.

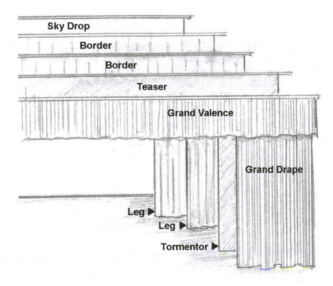

Stage drapes, front view

Drops are another series of soft goods used in scenery. Drops are traditionally large pieces of painted or colored canvas or muslin that provide large-scale backgrounds. They can be rigged to fly in and out if the theatre is so equipped. Usually, they are constructed with ties at the top seam so they can be easily attached to battens. The bottom hem may be equipped with a pocket for a pipe or chain that provides weight to help the drop hang flat and stay in place. Musical theatre tends to rely on a series of painted canvas drops to quickly move the story from one location to another. The **sky drop,** which is mounted upstage of the playing area to serve as background, is another common drop. Though now rare, a **cyclorama** may be used upstage in place of a sky drop with its extreme ends curving toward the apron to partially surround the playing space. **Cut drops** have a profiled edge to help layer an image such as tree foliage. A **portal** is a drop with its center section cut away to create a surface with a smaller opening than the natural proscenium. A **false proscenium** is often a hard-faced portal that has been constructed to replace or augment the look of a theatre's natural proscenium arch. A **show curtain** is a drop that may replace a main drape for a production and has been created as part of the scenic environment.

Drops often need special lighting to make them convincing illusions. Space might need to be allocated for a decorative **ground row,** which masks lights placed behind it to up-light a drop from the stage floor.

For Further Exploration

Carter, Paul. 1994. *The Backstage Handbook: An Illustrated Almanac of Technical Information.* Louisville, KY: Broadway Press.

B.A, Jay O. Glerum M. A. 2007. *Stage Rigging Handbook.* Carbondale: Southern Illinois University Press.

Stagehand Primer. n.d. Accessed August 16, 2018. http://www.ia470.com/primer/.

MODULE 6

Design and Collaboration

Where do design ideas come from? The best short answer: from the script! In the theatre, the script is our base material. When material is well chosen for your specific audience, your inspiration mostly comes from that script. The collaborative process begins once a group of theatre makers who comprise the **creative team** get together to discuss possibilities for their production. In preparation for this first meeting, sometimes referred to as a "design conference," each participant will have immersed themselves in the script and familiarized themselves with any and all references made to history, people, places, or cultures—anything that may be unfamiliar to them.

> **There's More to Know**
>
> Like to read? Creative team members read the script for a production many times. Each reading delivers new insights and new information about the story being told. Theatre makers must know not only the story, but also the workings of the way it is told in order to effectively deliver it to an audience. The first reading should be for pleasure and to let the script work on you. Take note of what surprised or moved you on the first reading, when you are as close to the audience's experience of the story as you will ever be. The second reading allows you to focus on the shape of the play, its imagery, and needs. Further readings will reveal more specific details about characters and story dynamics. The more you read, the clearer you will be about how you can effectively deliver the story to your audience.

Their homework done, the creative team can then discuss the themes within the play and the best way to help the audience experience the play and receive its message.

Early conversations involve thoughtful exchanges about these ideas, while also touching on production concerns such as timeline, budgetary realities, and cast size. Often the production's director speaks about what excites them about the script, a specific theme they want to showcase, or a vision for the production. Many designers take copious notes during the first meeting so they can be sure to consider all the ideas brought to the table by their collaborators. Some bring visual samples of images, colors, or textures they have responded to while reading and researching the script. The first meeting of a creative team is successful if everyone leaves with a clearer vision of how the production might take form.

After this first meeting, most designers go back to the script and read it again. They identify connections between the text and the ideas discussed in the meeting. Sometimes individual meetings with the director help the ideas progress. By the time a second meeting is called, the designers are usually able to bring a series of visual examples to illustrate the direction in which they have been moving. It is often the more tangible arts of scenery and costuming that are able to share visual representations of what the production might look like first. **Thumbnail sketches** of scenery and line renderings of costumes may be shared at this time. If the work presented is well received by the entire creative team, a sense of the style and concept for the production becomes clearer, and designs of more ephemeral elements such as light, sound, and movement can be expressed more distinctly against it. All of these considerations are eventually expressed as a **production concept,** which helps to unify the vision for the production. Aside from a production concept, color use for designs, stage mechanics, rehearsal scheduling, and budget allocation are also usually discussed at a second meeting.

There's More to Know

There are endless ways to represent the scenic needs of plays. Scenic designs are generally categorized by one of the following styles:

A *single set show:* A single environment supports the entire performance. Items may move within the setting, but the audience is not transported to another location through set changes. Often a three-wall interior setting is used. Such a setting is referred to as a "box set."

A *unit set show:* One setting serves for multiple locations with minor adjustments. A designer may find an overarching theme to represent, yet allow accommodations for small, specific elements required by scene locations.

A *multi-set show:* In this setting elements are changeable in order to transport the audience to a number of locations. Usually full stage changes are made, which often require both time and crews to facilitate.

After the second meeting, each designer goes to work on the support materials that accompany their designs. A scenic designer develops a set of drafted, scaled plans of the theatre space and the show design and sets of colored renderings or samples of color elements. A costume designer produces a series of **color renderings** of each costume and chooses **swatches** of fabric that represent the color and texture of the costume elements. A lighting designer prepares a series of drafted views that map where the lighting equipment will be placed, the color filters it will employ, and lists of the specific equipment required. Sound designers submit a map of the equipment locations and a list of cues to be supplied or created.

By the time designers have created the backup materials to communicate their designs, meetings with the technical director, costume shop manager, and master electrician are required to then plan the execution of the designs. This may take place in individual meetings between designers and area leads or may come in the form of a **production meeting**.

Production meetings continue throughout the production process. If possible, a weekly meeting is helpful. Many professional productions have fewer meetings because creative team members are often working from different cities until closer to technical rehearsals.

The designer's job is far from finished once they have submitted plans to the technical director. After plans are received, the process of determining the cost of realizing the design begins. Designers may be asked to alter or revise their plans to bring them into budget. Once a design has been deemed affordable, the designers begin to work closely with the shops to see that the details of the designs are realized appropriately. Daily communications from the rehearsal room also influence the design and sometimes require alterations to be made. The designer's role at this time is to shepherd the design through this part of the process.

Once construction is completed, the process of loading the design elements into the theatre space begins. Once again the designers are on hand to ensure all of the elements are in place and properly finished. During this time, the production may hold a **spacing rehearsal,** when the director and performers are given time to explore the realized elements, which until that time may have been represented in the rehearsal room with only tape lines and rough approximations of props and costume pieces.

After everything has been installed in the theatre space, the technical rehearsal process can begin. During this time, designers work with the stage manager and technical director to finalize the elements of the show and adapt the design for any new circumstances discovered at load-in or a spacing rehearsal. We have learned to expect that adjustments need to be made once everything comes together. We hope that if we have planned and communicated well, the changes needed are achievable in the amount of work time we have prior to opening. The designers, director, and management team work to pull all aspects of the production together in a way that is most effective for the audiences.

We are all storytellers, and the technical and dress rehearsal periods are our opportunity to ensure we are all telling a cohesive story to our audience. Following each rehearsal, there are usually daily sessions of **technical notes,** in which concerns and needs are communicated to the entire **company**. Often a separate session of notes is also held involving only the performers, director, and stage manager to discuss **acting notes**.

The final part of the process involves **preview performances**. Previews are test performances. They allow the production to gauge how an audience will interact with the performance. For instance, in a comedy it is very important to allow the audience a moment to laugh, but then to keep the show's pace moving forward. If a performer cuts off the audience's reaction by speaking too soon after a laugh line, then the audience is conditioned not to laugh for fear they will miss the dialogue being spoken onstage. A preview performance allows the performers and crew the opportunity to perfect the timing of the show. Traditionally tickets for preview performances are sold at a discounted rate. In most theatres, reviewers who might write about the production are not allowed to review a preview performance. During previews, designers continue to finesse their designs, while also learning from how the audience reacts to the work. Daily production meetings or note sessions continue through the preview period.

Once opening night has arrived, designers' services are no longer needed and most move on to the next project.

However, individually, designers should always take time to reflect on each production and evaluate their work, their choices, and the relative success of each.

For Further Exploration

Ingham, Rosemary. 1998. *From Page to Stage: How Theatre Designers Make Connections Between Scripts and Images*. Portsmouth, NH: Heinemann Drama.

"Theatre People | AACT." n.d. Accessed August 16, 2018. https://aact.org/theatre-people.

MODULE 7

Scenery and Construction

Scenery encompasses all the physical decorative elements of the stage design. It includes curtains, platforms, stairs, walls, furniture, and all of the other items a show might require for its visual environment. Scenic designs are delivered to the technical director as a set of plans for the design. The technical director drafts any additional "working drawings" necessary for construction and then distributes the scaled plans to the scene shop. Drafted plans are drawn in a "language of lines" and standard graphic symbols that are generally understood by those who need to interpret them. Each draft has a **title block** in one corner that tells you what the drawing represents and how to interpret its **scale** for construction, as well as who created it and when it was drafted or last revised.

Walls that we construct as **flats** and raised **platforms** that create **levels,** also referred to as **decks,** are the most commonly constructed elements for scenery. Of course there may be lots of other items that a scenic design utilizes or requires, but these elements are standards for set construction.

As scenery represents a large portion of the physical needs for a production, it is often the most labor intensive of the design elements and usually maes up a significant part of the budget. It stands to reason that the less you need to build from scratch, the more time and money can be saved or allocated to other production needs. **Stock scenery** items are those that the theatre stores between productions and can be reused, redressed, or altered for a production. Companies that have allocated space to store scenic elements such as flat walls and platforms can effectively and economically reuse them. Storage, therefore, is a premium in theatre spaces, and you usually find that something is stored in every nook and cranny of a theatre space in case it might be useful in the future. Environmentally, it also makes sense to reuse as much as possible because plays tend to have relatively short performance runs, and the art form could otherwise be seen as wasteful.

To be most useful, stock scenery should be constructed in sizes that are commonly required and can be assembled in a variety of configurations. Therefore, **stock sizes** of scenery are also common. Flat walls are generally constructed in 1-, 2-, 3-, or 4-foot widths. Heights are dependent on the most useful size for a given stage space.

Some flats can be 20-feet tall or taller, while the most common sizes are 8 feet, 10 feet, and 12 feet.

Flats are commonly constructed in two basic types. A **soft-cover flat** is constructed on a frame, usually of wood, but sometimes metal. A canvas is stretched over the entire plane that faces the audience. Much like a large painter's canvas, a flat can be painted to resemble any environment. Soft-cover flats are both lightweight and portable and have been traditional elements of scenery for hundreds of years. Each of the joints of the flat's frame is supported by a thin plywood brace. These **corner blocks** and **keystones** help to stiffen the relatively thin flat frames. These frames, often constructed of 1-by-3- or 1-by-4-inch lumber, are economical to construct and their minimal thickness (approximately 1 inch each) reduces storage space. However, their relative delicacy due to the soft-cover makes them an unpopular choice in modern theatre. While there was a time when it was standard for performers to act in front of the scenery, modern plays require them to interact with the scenery, making canvas walls impractical.

Hard-cover flats are also commonly built as wooden frames, but their face is covered in a thin plywood rather than canvas. This makes them more durable, but also heavier and generally more expensive to construct. The most common version of a hard-cover flat is the "studio" or "Broadway" style flat. These frames are not only stiffer than other styles, but their depth also allows them to be easily secured to one another as well as to the floor. If your production requires actors to lean on the set's walls or throw things against them, a hard-cover flat is your best choice.

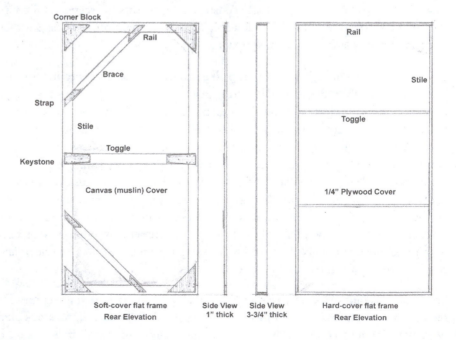

Flat frames

Flats are sometimes constructed in shapes other than rectangles. If a flat is constructed to have a shaped edge profile, we refer to it as a **profile flat**. Tree shapes and arches are common profile flats. Flats can be propped up by triangular frames called **jacks** where needed for support.

Platforms are often constructed as frames that support a full sheet of plywood as their top **skin** surface, or lid. In the U.S., plywood is sold in sheets that measure 4 feet by 8 feet, and so platforms are constructed this size or smaller. Groups of stock platforms can be assembled into larger **decks** of stage levels with support legs that set their heights above the **natural stage floor**. A **facing** can be added to these platforms that hides the legs so they appear as solid block shapes to the audience.

Typical framing for a wooden theatrical platform can be constructed from either 2-by-4 or 1-by-6-inch boards. Framed on-edge, both materials provide the necessary support the plywood lid requires. Joists that span the 4-foot width of the frame need to be installed on 24-inch **centers** in order to provide the stiffness and weight distribution required for the platform to safely support scenery and performers. A stage platform is typically skinned in ¾-inch thick plywood and supported by a minimum of six legs. Metal platform frames are also common to large productions and touring shows.

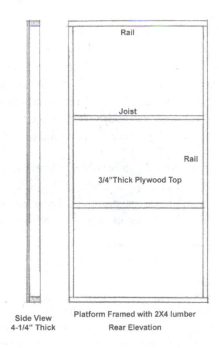

Side View
4-1/4" Thick

Platform Framed with 2X4 lumber
Rear Elevation

Wood framed platform with plywood lid

If we add levels to our stages, we need stairs to get from one height to another. Humans have an interesting relationship with stairs. Most of us do not need to carefully navigate each rise in a staircase, but instead have an autopilot feature that usually allows us to climb or descend them with ease. This is true until one stair is of a slightly different **rise** than the rest, then we are apt to trip and fall at this step. Designers should take care to ensure, as much as possible, that all of the stairs on a given set are of the same height so the actors can traverse them easily without great concentration. Many theatres keep stock stair units as a part of their inventory.

There's More to Know

When constructing stairs for a set, it is helpful to use the 18-inch rule for your calculations. The rise of each tread to the next and the run or depth of each tread when added together should add up to 18 inches. Therefore, if a 6-inch rise from tread to tread is required, then your run or depth of tread should be 12 inches. If your rise is 8 inches per tread, then your stairs should each have a 10-inch run depth. This will keep the natural rhythm of human movement intact.

Plywood and other **sheet goods** are important building materials for scenic construction. Plywood are made up of sheets of material that have been manufactured as a strata of layers, or "veneers." These thin layers of wood have been peeled off long logs and then laid in a stack with the **wood grain** of each layer running perpendicular to the layer above and below. As wood is strongest along its grain fibers, crossing the grains adds strength to the ply. These layers are pressed and glued together, making for a very strong sheet of lumber. More layers add thickness to the ply, making it capable of supporting a greater load. Theatrical platforms are generally skinned with a sheet of plywood at least ¾-inch thick to support the weight of the actors and scenery. Sheet goods also include decorative items such as paneling and materials like MDF (medium density fiberboard), which are not good materials to support weight, but have other qualities that can be useful in construction. Generally, in the United States, sheet goods are sold in panels of 4 feet by 8 feet.

Plywood is graded based on both the finish of its outermost veneers and the quality of the woods that make up its inner plies. If you want a smooth sanded surface with no mars to the wood grain, you need to purchase higher-grade plywood. Low-grade plywood may have "holidays," or holes, in their veneers, including the exterior layers.

Interior Grade	Face	Back	Inner Plies	Use and Appearance
A-A	A	A	C	Cabinet doors, furniture where both sides show. Good natural wood finish both sides.
A-B	A	B	C	Paneling, one-sided natural wood finish. Finished face; smooth, sanded back.
A-C	A	C	C	Platforms/work seen from one side only. Finish grade face, voids on back.

Common plywood grade chart

Consider This

To glue or not to glue? It is a good question. If you are constructing stock scenery that has elements that will either take abuse or have questionable safety or stability, then YES, glue. If, however, the construction is decorative, and you want to recoup the materials for later use, then glue will only make the job harder.

Modern scenery includes many of the architectural elements and details we use every day, like appliances that need to work, windows that will be opened, or a sink with running water. These are called **practical**. Doors are the most common practical element of scenery. They often need to function normally, but also stand up to some abuse called for by the script, which can range from hard knocking to full forced entry attempts. It can be a challenge for carpenters to support and reinforce these elements within an environment of temporarily constructed flat walls.

Many scripts call for a variety of locations to be represented within the same play. Scene designers work to find ways to transport their audience from one location to another without taking massive breaks in the action to achieve the changes. A number of rolling platform elements, known as **wagons,** can help streamline these transitions by transporting large props and scenery on and off the stage quickly. A variety of wagons are common to scenic design. A large turntable wagon that can spin to reveal a new setting is called a **revolve**. Some theatres are equipped with a built-in revolve that is permanently installed as part of their stage floor. Platform wagons that pivot onstage from a fixed point in the wings are called **jackknife platforms**. **Straight run platform wagons** roll either upstage to downstage or in and out of the wings. The wheels that these wagons operate on, known as casters, are either **fixed casters** or **swivel casters**. A fixed caster can only roll along a straight path, while swivel casters allow units to be rolled in any direction. Sometimes these wagons are guided by a track built into the stage floor.

Scenery construction methods and choice of materials vary from theatre to theatre, but standards for construction are important for every company. Standard construction methods greatly increase safety and reliability, and items built-in the same manner tend to fit together easily without modifications.

Many theatres work primarily in wood, which is relatively inexpensive and malleable. Some shops work in metals as well, though separate working spaces are often required for metal construction due to the inherent fire danger. Simple theatrical construction does not typically involve intensive wood joinery, but instead relies on abutted joint, or **butt joint,** construction methods. When working with lumber, it is important to understand the "true" or actual dimensions of the lumber in order to correctly figure the lengths needed to be cut for a project. Lumber is sold by what we refer to as a **nominal dimension**. Nominal dimensions are the sizes to which each piece of lumber was rough cut at the mill. The lumber we buy at our local supplier has then been put through a series of finishing machines that have cut the lumber into consistent rectangular planks and sanded away the rough edges. This process removes some of the wood and leaves us with a piece whose actual dimension is significantly smaller than its nominal dimension. Scene shops regularly work with sticks of lumber we refer to as "one-by-three" to build flat frames, but the carpenters must remember those pieces actually measure ¾ inch by 2½ inch.

Nominal Lumber Dimensions	Actual Lumber Dimensions
1X3	¾" x 2½"
1X4	¾" x 3½"
1x6	¾" x 5½"
1X8	¾" x 7¼"
1x12	¾" x 11¼"
2x4	1½" x 3½"
2x6	1½" x 5½"
2x8	1½" x 7¼"
4x4	3½" x 3½"

Common plank lumber sizes

Woodworking requires a series of cutting and assembly tools. These tools must be well-maintained and their safety recommendations upheld in order to ensure a safe working environment. All construction tools are potentially dangerous. They are loud, and to a new user, often seem scary. Before you use any construction tools, make sure you have been adequately trained and are aware of all personal safety precautions and equipment required for your task.

Consider This

The theatre is a potentially dangerous environment. Many factors contribute to this. We build temporary scenery, hang lighting equipment next to fabric curtains, run lots of extension cords, hang many things overhead, and then we work amongst it all in relative darkness during performances. That means we need to be extra careful to take all possible precautions to work safely. Wear provided safety equipment. Read product warnings. Keep a clean work environment and always stay aware of the work happening around you.

The wood working tools in use at most scene shops fall into two categories. "Stationary tools," which are permanently placed in the shop with adequate working space around them. Table saws and cut-off saws such as a tilting arbor (chop saw) or sliding arbor saw are common to most wood shops. A drill press, sanding station, lathe, and band saws are also common. The second category of tools is "hand tools."

These are familiar tools such as hammers, wrenches, and screwdrivers, but also include hand-held power tools like circular saws, sabre saws, and reciprocating saws as well as grinders, staplers, and driver drills.

Common shop tools

Table saw: Used primarily for ripping lumber (cutting along the grain). Allows for wood to be beveled on a tilting arbor table saw.

Cut-off saw: Used primarily for crosscutting lumber against the grain. Can be a tilting arbor saw.

Band saw: A saw with a continuous loop blade. Allows for the cutting of curves along material.

Drill press: A stationary tool in which a drill motor can be lowered into and lifted from materials providing an opportunity for precise holes to be drilled.

Pneumatic stapler: An air-driven stapler. Drive staples from ½-inch lengths up to 2½-inch lengths

Driver drill: A cordless, battery-driven drill that has an adjustable clutch to assist in the insertion of screws.

Unless you are constructing stock scenery, most theatrical construction is temporary. It must be safe and durable, but after the show closes, we would like to recoup as much of the material as possible for reuse. Using screws as a primary fastener allows us to construct and deconstruct with little damage to the materials. Battery-powered driver drills have made the use of screws rather than nails or staples a reasonable alternative for construction. **Drywall screws**, which are hard and sharp, have become widely used in theatre construction because they are faster to work with than woodscrews and have better adhesion than nails. However, they are brittle and are can be prone to breaking.

Nuts and bolts are also heavily used for theatre construction. A wide variety of bolts are available. **Carriage bolts** and **hex bolts** are the most common to theatre.

Fastener chart

For Further Exploration

Raoul, Bill. 1998. *Stock Scenery Construction: A Handbook.* Louisville, KY: Broadway Press.

International Alliance of Theatrical Stage Employees. n.d. Accessed August 16, 2018. http://www.iatse.net/.

Props and Effects

Properties, or "props," are crucial design elements for stage productions. Anything an actor handles, carries, or manipulates that is not attached to the walls or floors is considered a stage prop. Because actors interact with props, they are also elements that the audience often pays close attention to. They are highly visible and equally important to storytelling, so careful attention must be paid to their selection and function.

Stage props are broken down into several categories. The first is **set props**. Set props include furniture and large-scale elements that may be moved by an actor or technician during the show. The second category of properties is **set dressings,** also known as "decorative props." Set dressings include items such as wall art, window curtains, and shelves of books. These items are decorative in nature and are not typically handled during the performance. The final categories are **hand props** and **personal props**. Hand props are handled by performers and can be almost anything from something as simple as a pencil, to something more complex like a weapon, to anything in between. Hand props must be durable enough to be used throughout the technical rehearsals and run of a production. They must also be easy to use for the actor or technician who operates them. Personal props are a subset of hand props and are items of a personal nature that enhance a character. Often these items are chosen in concert with the costume designer. Sometimes personal props stay with the actors costume and are always carried by the actor during the production. These items include things such as cigarettes and lighters, wallets, combs, and parasols.

Some play scripts include a **properties list** of items needed for production. Often, this list is reprinted from a professional production and includes the properties from that incarnation of the show. If a list is not provided, one can be created through a careful close reading of the script, noting each item required for the scenes. Prop lists of this type are created by the scenic designer or, if involved, a prop designer. Once a list of required items has been made, any research needed to clarify the look and function of items can be done. Many plays take place at a certain historical period of time. We refer to this as "period drama." If your play recreates the feeling of an historic era onstage, then many of your prop elements could be things that you are unfamiliar with. They are also likely to be much harder to find than a modern item. Period props may have to be researched and built from scratch rather than located.

Even if all of the needed items are commonly available, most props used in a live production have been altered in some way to make them "stage worthy." Plays tend to be written about extraordinary moments in the lives of their characters, moments in which the characters are on the precipice of some great undertaking or struggle. In these moments the characters often behave extraordinarily. They stand on chairs, slam doors, throw glassware, or dance on tables. The props of the show must be able to withstand this unusual usage, show after show. Chairs, tables, and other household items are often reinforced for stage use. Remember, borrowed items must be well cared for and alterations to them may not be possible.

Consider This

Several types of prop artisans are common to the theatre. Each individual has a special skill and methodology for the creation or acquisition and delivery of the needed items for a production. Often props can be purchased for a show from retailers, thrift stores, and online sources. Some prop masters are brilliant at sourcing items and can find whatever may be required. These people tend to be great researchers and will search tirelessly for items they need. Others are builders and will likely try to create the bulk of the required items. These artists are masters of a wide variety of materials, construction techniques, and paint effects. All prop masters must have strong organizational skills. Prop tracking lists can be very complex, and constant communication with the rehearsal room and shops about the evolving needs for props is vital.

The scenic designer and props designer provide visual research to the director and prop artisans for planned props. During the rehearsal process, actors are given approximations of the show props that will be used for performances in order for them to become familiar with those items and incorporate them into their performances. These **rehearsal props** should mimic the actual intended prop as closely as possible in scale, weight, and function. Prop masters usually do not include actual show props in rehearsal rooms for fear of loss or damage. Rehearsal props are naturally subject to some abuse as the actors actively explore their potential use in the production.

Once the needed props have been established, collected, and altered for stage use, they are ready to be used in technical rehearsals. Props are set out, maintained, cleaned, and stored by the prop crew or backstage run crew. Usually, long tables are set backstage near entrances and exits and props are arranged on these tables for quick access by cast and crew. These tables can be covered in butcher paper so props can be kept track of by drawing a line around them and labeling the place on the table where they sit. Further organization can be achieved by using tape to outline sections of the table and labeling them by scene or by actor. This system allows for all items to be placed in the same area for easy location and identification as well as provide visual shorthand to recognize any missing items from the table prior to a performance. Once props have been set for a performance, both the stage manager and the actors perform a "prop check" to visually check to ensure everything needed is ready to go.

There's More to Know

Common prop elements such as glassware, silverware, and dishes must be carefully washed after each performance so that germs are not passed among the cast. Items like pipes or cigarette holders should be carefully labeled so they are not shared by multiple performers. All food and beverages should be refrigerated to keep them fresh and safe. In addition, people working on a production are often subject to health issues as they are getting enough rest and are stressed during production periods. Anything you can do to keep everyone healthy is a worthwhile investment.

Food and drink props are common to the theatre. The prop master should ask the stage manager to survey the entire cast who touch or eat any food or drink props, or **consumables,** to discover any dietary restrictions and allergies. Whatever is ultimately chosen for the food prop seen onstage needs to be something that no one will have a negative reaction to and can be kept hot or cold accordingly and handled safely for each performance.

The term "consumable" can also be applied to anything used up or destroyed during a performance such as burning letters or blank ammunition that is fired. Confetti is also considered a consumable. Breaking down these items into their own subcategory helps us to track amounts required and the cost of these items for each performance as well as for the entire rehearsal period and run of shows.

There's More to Know

Blank-firing weapons are guns that have had their barrel plugged and are not able to be loaded with a live round. These weapons are available in many styles and calibers to match common and period weapons. All replica weapons must be treated with respect and great care. Theatres should have a procedure in place for exactly how the weapon will be used and accounted for. Weapons should be kept under lock and key as much as possible, and only personnel who need to handle the weapon should be allowed to do so. Although a piece of blank ammunition does not have a bullet as a projectile, it is still a controlled explosion occurring in the chamber of the weapon and may propel it's wadding and other debris at the speed of a bullet. When this explosion occurs, an envelope of hot gas and burning powder flashes out in all directions from the barrel, creating potential danger for anyone in proximity to the weapon. Blank loads are also very loud. The hearing of anyone in proximity to the weapon when fired should be protected.

Weapons are also prop-based special effects that need special care and attention. They are common to many theatre productions, and, although they have always been dangerous items to manage, the current problems facing our society in regards to public shootings have made even handling a plastic replica gun a danger for any public performance. When a blank-firing weapon is used on stage, specific training for the *entire company* occurs in order to ensure that everyone knows how to stay safe around such an effect. It should also be said that a weapon capable of holding a *live* round rather than a blank should NEVER be used in a production. Other weapons such as swords, daggers, and even kitchen knives should always have their edges dulled and tips blunted for general safety.

Special effects are associated with props. Often special effects rely on motors and machinery, and so they are also considerations for the set and lighting designer. Common theatre special effects include atmospheric effects such as theatrical fog and haze and practical effects such as snow, rain, and fire.

The responsibilities of special effects are often shared between several production departments. Water effects such as rain, ponds, showers, and sinks often involve the master electrician, both for the installation of associated electrical equipment for pumps, filters, and heaters, but also, from a safety standpoint, their expertise is needed as water and electricity don't mix well and can add up to significant danger. When needed, a constant pressure flow to practical faucets might be accomplished via a hose to an existing water source or by creating a closed pressurized system by using a garden sprayer.

Weather-based effects have been used in theatre for many years. Thunder, though now usually recreated with a recorded sound effect, was traditionally created using a "thunder sheet," a large sheet of thin metal that was struck or distorted to produce the sound. Practical rain can be accomplished by a system that is essentially an overhead sprinkler system. However, containing and circulating water is a tricky undertaking and has huge implications for electrical safety.

Fire effects are another area that requires specific expertise to produce a reliable and safe effect. Any live flame likely requires a special permit to be granted by your local fire marshal. Permits for small naked flames, such as those from a candle, match, or cigarette lighter, are reasonably common requests, and depending on your specific production, may be fairly easy to acquire if the proper conditions and procedures are met. LED candles and battery operated torches and fire effects have become quite convincing and are commonly available as practical and safe alternatives to live flame. Audiences today are often very put off by smoking of any kind onstage. They have become very accepting of miming smoking without ever actually lighting a prop cigarette. Non-nicotine e-cigarettes can also be a convincing alternative.

Unlike rain, snow is a fairly easy effect to achieve onstage with convincing results. A **snow cradle** is rigged from a batten above the effect area. The cradle is then manipulated to drop a snow-like substance. Depending on your needs, a manufactured snowflake product made from plastic, Styrofoam beads (static causes these to stick to everything), or even dried potato flakes could be used. Snow cradles are also often used to drop flower petals or confetti. Snow machines that produce miniature soap bubbles are also convincing, but the collected soap can be slippery on the stage floor.

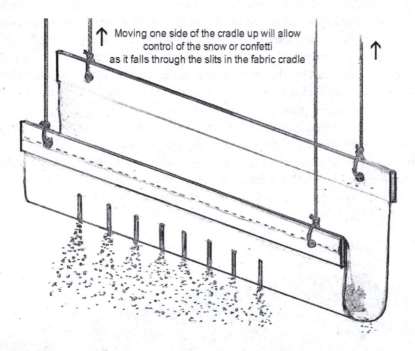

A simple fabric snow cradle

Breakaway props like **sugar-glass** bottles or glassware are common for fight scenes and are commercially available. These props require careful planning with the performers to keep everyone safe. The production needs to order enough of these expendable items for sufficient experimentation and practice. It is possible for an experienced prop artisan to make custom sugar-glass items for a production, but it has become an expensive and time-consuming endeavor.

Consider This

When glassware is required onstage, it is often advisable to use a plastic or acrylic alternative to actual, breakable glass. Unless you are "clinking" glasses, they will be convincing replacements and can prevent what otherwise can be both a safety hazard and a time-consuming cleanup onstage.

Breakaway furniture and collapsing crates may be made either from a soft wood such as balsa, or can be pre-broken and held together lightly so actors won't be injured by their impact. Many extra breakaway objects should be kept on standby and for rehearsals.

Productions using weaponry or breakaway props and furniture also require an expert in **stage combat** to work with the cast and crew to carefully plan the actions involved so they are convincing for the audience as well as repeatable and safe.

Atmospheric effects, such as fog, smoke, and haze, have become very common to in productions. Theatrical fog can be produced in several ways. Fog machines that vaporize a liquid by heating it are used frequently. These units are safe, reliable, and inexpensive to run. This type of fog can be run through a cooling unit, which allows it to hang or drop toward the floor rather than rise as a vapor. Dry ice (CO_2) can be employed to create a cool fog that falls and hugs the stage floor. Liquid nitrogen can also be used to produce a pressurized fog effect that can be useful for magic appearances. Smoke and **smoke machines** are often used as interchangeable terms with fog, though smoke effects should accurately be categorized as pyrotechnic effects. Haze is used to thicken the stage atmosphere. It allows the lighting instruments' beams to be seen. The look of a rock concert is achieved through the use of haze. **Hazer** units are similar to fog machines but continuously put out a light vapor distributed over a large area.

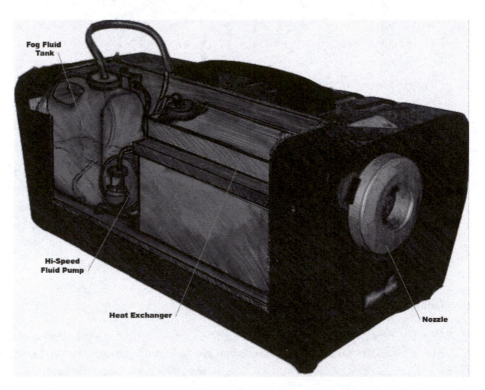

A fog machine

For Further Exploration

James, Thurston. 1987. *The Theater Props Handbook: A Comprehensive Guide to Theater Properties, Materials, and Construction.* White Hall: Betterway Publications.

"Instructables - How to Make Anything." n.d. Instructables.Com. Accessed August 16, 2018. https://www.instructables.com/.

MODULE 9

Stage Management

If you want to be at the center of everything and carry a great amount of responsibility and pressure, then you probably aspire to be a stage manager. The stage manager can be one of the first people to be brought on board for a production. They may become involved around the same time the **creative team** is assembled and begin by scheduling the initial meetings for a new production, which allows them to be involved with the entire production process. Or, they may be brought in just prior to the beginning of rehearsals. Regardless of when a stage manager's time with a production begins, their responsibilities and focus throughout the life of the production will go through a series of changes.

In this collaborative art of theatre, careful coordination of all of the constituent elements is crucial for success. Managing the schedules and communication of all the people involved in the production is one of the most complicated parts of the stage manager's job. From designers to crews, producers to performers, house staff to ushers, the flow of communication between individuals is central to the production. Facilitating this communication is by no means the only responsibility a stage manager assumes, but it is representative of the special glue that this person provides to a production. Coordination of calendars and schedules for an entire company is an increasingly difficult task in our modern society, yet we all must be there in the room to make this art happen. The creation of a **rehearsal calendar** often falls to the stage manager. To help facilitate communication among the company, the stage manager publishes a **contact sheet** listing each member of the company, their role in the production, and their contact information. Stage managers also frequently run the **auditions** by scheduling the actors, collecting their contact information and schedules, and ensuring everyone gets needed breaks to work at their best. Once casting decisions have been made, all rehearsal and performance schedule conflicts must be addressed, and the stage manager publishes a final rehearsal schedule along with a complete contact sheet.

As a central figure in contact with all aspects of the production, the stage manager is uniquely suited to see that something only communicated to some may need to be passed on to others who will also be affected. The best way to achieve this clarity is to always communicate through the stage manager (or at least always copy them on your communication). Think of a bicycle wheel representing communication. If the company members are the spokes along the outer rim, the stage manager is at the center hub. All of the communication coming into the center and then distributed out to all concerned. For instance, if the director decides to have a performer sit in a seat in the audience, the stage manager knows this must be coordinated with the box office so a ticket for that seat is not sold for any performance. In addition, stage managers know the lighting designer needs to be aware if actors will be performing in a nontraditional acting area.

Often the members of the creative team finalizes their designs for a production around the time a play is cast. Prior to the first rehearsal, the stage manager needs to ask the designers for copies of plans and designs to facilitate the rehearsal process. The main plan required is a scaled **ground plan** of the stage design. The stage manager uses this plan to lay out a series of tapelines on the floor of the rehearsal space that represent key elements of the stage design. Tapelines stand in for walls, doors, windows, stairs, and major furniture elements. Often the rehearsal space is not as large as the stage space, and decisions about what and how to best represent the design may need to be made.

There's More to Know

Laying out a tape plan for rehearsals on stage or on the rehearsal space floor requires a scaled ground plan from the set designer. This plan will be drawn to scale and may be ¼-inch, ½-inch, or another scale set. It is standard practice for the set designer to provide a "measured plan" which lists key measurements and minimizes the amount of scale measurements a stage manager needs to interpret. When laying out a space, corners and intersections are measured from the centerline of the stage. This reference line runs down the center of the stage from the upstage wall to the downstage edge of the stage. Measuring from the centerline helps ensure the elements are laid out proportionately in the space.

A scale rule is a specialized ruler that measures in a variety of scales. It is normally a triangular ruler that reads on each face from each direction allowing for 12 scales to be represented on one ruler. Architectural rather than engineering scales are used for theatre.

After organizing initial meetings with the design team, the stage manager must look forward into the process as ideas are solidified for the production's design. If the costume designer advances the idea that the central character will have many wardrobe changes during the performance, the stage manager can be thinking ahead about the number of backstage dressing crew needed to run the show. If special effects are being considered, the stage manager looks closely at the technical rehearsal schedule to ensure the necessary time is built-in to rehearse these elements. If the production uses actors who are unionized, the stage manager (who is usually represented by the same union) looks out for elements such as **raked stages** or atmospheric effects like fog—the use of which is regulated by the union contract. During this phase, a stage manager's role is to be supportive of the creative team, while at the same time informing them of the consequences of production choices.

Often a **design presentation** is scheduled for the company around the time of the first rehearsal so the creative team can describe designs to the cast.

There's More to Know

Recording the blocking (actors' movements) is an important function of the stage manager. During rehearsals, the company may try multiple traffic patterns before they settle on the correct movement for the production. It can be difficult to remember the option chosen, and a record of the movement is vital. You can also imagine that because blocking is changed repeatedly, it must be recorded in pencil so that it can be updated throughout the rehearsal period. Stage managers tend to use a shorthand notation to record blocking in the relatively small margins of the script pages. A key to their notations should be kept with the prompt book so others can read the notations. Software is now available to facilitate blocking notation.

You will probably need to abbreviate all of the characters' names as well as common movements and actions. An example of some shorthand notation might be:

ENT	Enter
EXT	Exit
✕	Cross
→	toward
◡	Cross DS of
◠	Cross US of
⤴	Stand
⤵	Sit
⅄	Kneel
P/U	Pick Up
P/P	Put Down
⊤⊤	Table
ꜧ	Chair

During the rehearsal process, the stage manager ensures a safe and productive work environment, breaks are taken as needed, and records both the blocking of the actors and notes of the rehearsal so as the show's needs develop, all affected parties can adjust to support those needs. Daily **rehearsal reports** are sent to the production team with information and questions to keep the show on track.

During the rehearsal process, the creative team is invited to see a few rehearsals so they can see how the show is progressing. The first of these invited rehearsals is commonly called a **stumble-through**. This rehearsal occurs soon after the entire show has been blocked, and the actors try their best to represent all of the movement in the rehearsal so designers can get a sense of the shape of the show, of how the set is used, and, for the lighting designer, where people stand. Later, as the show continues to progress and develop, **run-throughs** are scheduled so designers can see the progress again prior to technical rehearsals.

Toward the end of the rehearsal process, it is common for productions to incorporate sound into the rehearsal room. The playback of cues and music is handled by the stage manager and allows a better integration of sonic elements prior to technical rehearsals. It may also allow the stage manager to record sound element cues into their **prompt book**.

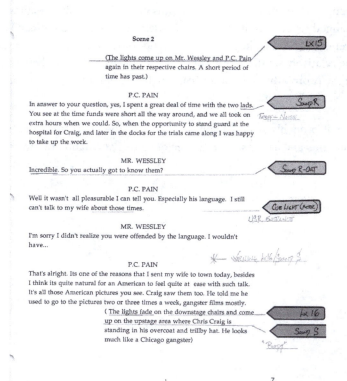

Prompt book page sample

In order to make sure the stage manager has all the various cues recorded in their prompt book, some more complicated productions may require a **paper tech** session, when the director and designers are present to talk through and coordinate the placement and timing of **cue** sequences for the production. These cues are fine-tuned during the actual technical rehearsals, but may need to be discussed in advance to make the most of the time in the theatre with a full production staff. In addition to the actual cues called to make changes in lighting, sound, and shifting scenery (also: video, spotlights, effects, music), the stage manager places warning cues in their prompt book so crew who have been idle for long periods of time are made aware they have a cue coming up soon.

There's More to Know

Cue light systems have become standard for many theatres. This system of colored lights allows a stage manager to communicate "warning," "stand-by," and "go" commands to both actors and technicians without audible communication. Lights are placed backstage in areas visible to those needing the cue, and a relay station in the stage manager's booth allows them to turn each light on and off.

After the sets and lights have been loaded into the theatre, several special rehearsals and showings may be scheduled. A **spacing rehearsal** might be scheduled to allow actors to become familiar with the set. A **lighting rehearsal** may be called in which the lighting designer shows a director preset cues or "looks" without the performers being present. A **costume parade** may be scheduled to see each character in their wardrobe under the stage lights for final adjustments. A **sitzprobe** may be scheduled for a musical performance wherein the cast and orchestra rehearse together in the performance space (most often seated) without following show blocking.

Prior to technical rehearsals, the stage manager ensures all prop tables are set up and labeled, headsets are available for crew as needed, adequate safety lighting is available backstage, and amenities such as fresh water and off-stage chairs are set for the cast.

The technical rehearsal process requires the stage manager to change their focus from the protected environment of the rehearsal room to the busy and complicated environment of the performance space. They are now in charge of the stage crew as well as the cast and have the design team on site finalizing their work as well. Timing is usually tight with much to be accomplished. Many of the people now involved have never seen this production in rehearsal, do not know the cast, and need to be led through a process that involves a great deal of communication. Much of this communication is accomplished over a **headset system** rather than face-to-face. All of these elements must become coordinated into a working unit, and this is the new focus of the stage manager. Again, clear communication is crucial in this process.

Some productions conduct a two-part technical rehearsal process beginning with a **dry tech**, when the performers are not present, allowing the crew to become familiar with the elements they control and to rehearse their cues and shifts with stand-ins as needed to represent the cast. The next step is a **wet tech,** which incorporates the actors. There is certainly value in separating these rehearsals, especially if there are many shifts in a show or when safety is of particular concern. Other companies may begin with a wet tech, incorporating everyone at once. This choice makes more sense if the actors actually help move items in transitions or if many costume changes are integral to the performance.

Once the technical rehearsals are complete and the cues and shifts are established and properly recorded into the prompt book, the production moves into **dress rehearsals**. The stage manager's focus must adjust again. Now the entire company is engaged, and rehearsals begin to run as if they were public performances. Actors inhabit dressing rooms, calls to places are made over intercom systems and backstage monitors, and everyone works in every corner of the theatre space. The stage manager keeps all of these individuals focused and on schedule. The stage manager now takes the reins in hand to drive the performance, calling all the cues, breaks, and, if necessary, **holds**. They also continue to produce daily reports of all rehearsal activity.

Many companies hold **preview performances** prior to the official opening of a production. These previews allow the company to adjust to the presence of the audience. They can be especially important in establishing comic timing. Over a preview period it is common for the company to hold work sessions during the day to continue to refine the performance and to incorporate adjustments based on the public's response from these shows. During this time, the stage manager again switches focus from operation to rehearsal and then back to operation.

Once the show officially opens, the stage manager's focus shifts again. The director's contract is often at an end, and the stage manager now becomes responsible not only for running the show, but also for maintaining the integrity of the production. It is the stage manager's new responsibility to ensure the production looks and sounds the same on the 400th performance as it did on opening night. If an actor or operator begins to stray from that performance, it is the stage manager's job to let them know they need to come back to the work that was set by the director. Actors and stage managers are represented by the same trade union to clarify this role, which might seem disciplinary within a company. Sometimes a stage manager is called upon to run **put-in rehearsals** for replacement performers who take over roles in a running production.

During all performances the stage manager checks to ensure the stage space is safe, all necessary elements are functioning and in place, all personnel are accounted for, and the show is generally ready to entertain its audience. A half-hour before the show's start time, the stage manager makes a series of announcements to the company letting them know how long they have prior to **places call**. If required, the stage manager also runs a **fight call** to ensure actor safety prior to opening the house to the public.

Once a performance has concluded, the stage manager checks in with all departments to ensure everything is prepped for the next show. Costume repairs or any other needed work is scheduled so things will be in place for the next performance. When a show closes at the end of its run, the stage manager normally prepares the prompt book and all notes on running the production for the theatre's archives.

For Further Exploration

Ionazzi, Daniel. 1992. *The Stage Management Handbook*. White Hall: Betterway Books.

Kelly, Thomas A. 2009. *The Back Stage Guide to Stage Management, 3rd Edition: Traditional and New Methods for Running a Show from First Rehearsal to Last Performance*. New York: Back Stage Books.

"Actors' Equity Association." n.d. Accessed August 16, 2018. http://www.actorsequity.org.

MODULE 10

Costumes and Character Creation

From the time an actor first enters the stage the audience should be able to tell quite a lot about their character, even before they speak. The actor themselves, through posture, stance, gait, and general demeanor can communicate much, but their costume, much like our own clothes, establishes a lot of what the audience infers about that person at first glance. Humans make quick judgments about new stimulus from the world around us. Interpreting situations and reacting to things quickly helps to keep us safe, and, therefore, we are creatures who depend on generalizations that shortcut our perception to reaction time. We see a character hunched over and walking with the aid of a cane, and we assume them to be aged. If we are presented with someone in a white lab coat, we assume they are a scientist or doctor. Likewise, someone dressed in bright colors may seem outgoing, while someone dressed drably may seem more introverted. In our daily lives we develop our own characters as we choose how we present ourselves to the world, and our wardrobe is a key component of that presentation. Costume design is the artful creation of wardrobe that tells the stories of the play's characters. Good costume design accomplishes the looks required by the production while preserving the comfort and flexibility of the performers and addresses wardrobe maintenance concerns for the run of the production. It is an art that relies on knowledge of period detail, fabric construction, tailoring, and costume craft.

Theatrical costume designers are often responsible for the entire look of the character, including wardrobe, accessories, hairstyles (or wigs), and makeup. In some productions, a wig designer or makeup designer is involved. Initial costume designs are typically established prior to a full cast being selected for the show and may be revised to fit the body types of actors eventually cast for the production. Designs are usually rendered in a full-body sketch, which is either painted or otherwise colored to show the eventual desired look. Costume designers carefully consider the use of color and texture and coordinate them with the other stage designs. The **costume renderings** are often accompanied by a series of small pieces of the fabrics to be used in the construction of the costumes. These samples, called **swatches,** are also good for communicating the textures of the fabrics. Fabric textures give the other designers a sense of weight and how the costumes will be affected by light. The feel of fabrics is important to a design. The way a fabric drapes over a form is affected by this feel, which is referred to as the **hand** of the fabric.

There's More to Know

Fabrics can be classified in two basic categories: natural fabrics and synthetics. The "hand," or feel, of these two classifications of fabric as well as their performance qualities can be quite different and partially depends on how the threads or filaments are woven.

"Warp" and "weft" refer to the two directions fabric is woven in; the warp is the longitudinal threads, and the weft or filler runs perpendicular to it. Fabrics are woven on looms and fall into several main patterns: plain weave, satin weave, and twill. Woven fabrics tend to stretch only along their bias, or diagonally across the weave, unless woven of an elastic thread.

Fabrics can also be knit. Knit fabrics are constructed from a single length of thread, much like hand knitting. These fabrics allow stretch, or "give," in all directions.

Like other designers, costumers find their inspiration through a combination of careful close reading of the play script and research into the period style and customs for the wardrobe. A costumer may choose a high collared dress for an uptight matronly character, while a childlike bride-to-be may be in a flowing and unstructured gown. Whatever is chosen, it is designed to both allow the performer to move effectively and to inform the audience members about the kind of person they are watching. Costumes regularly establish a sense of class, age, sex, profession, country of origin, health, marital status, season, and sometimes morality.

A costume shop

Once a designer has created the renderings that the costume shop, or costume production facility, will build the wardrobe, a meeting with the costume shop staff will help to determine how production and maintainance of the wardrobe will be accomplished. A costume shop manager runs the costume shop. Assisted by the **first hand**, the costume shop manager shepherds the process of creating the wardrobe, ordering materials, and assigning work within the shop. Many costume shop managers are active workers in the shop and may specialize in one of several wardrobe construction methods. The two most common methods for creating wardrobe are **flat-patterning** and **draping**. Both require skill sets that are so different in approach that it can be rare to find someone who is highly accomplished at both. A pattern maker may create patterns for a show's wardrobe from scratch or may alter commercial patterns for fit or period details. Sometimes a piece of historic wardrobe is deconstructed to create a pattern from the pieces. A **cutter** is the term for someone who works with flat patterns and cuts the needed pieces of cloth from the bolt. If an existing pattern is being used for the garment, the cutter's job is to carefully follow that pattern to construct the piece. Cutters are skilled three-dimensional thinkers who understand fabric construction methods.

Alternatively, sometimes the style of costumes cannot be created using a pattern, like a toga or other diaphanous and flowing dress style. A **draper** creates these costumes by wrapping fabric over a dress form and then pining the fabric so it can be sewn to hold the desired shape.

Draped costumes on dress forms

At the initial shop meeting with the costume designer, the shop can begin to devise a schedule for creating the costumes based on decisions about what items will be built from scratch, what may be pulled from stock and altered, and what may be rented or purchased. As the look of each character's costume is usually communicated via a single rendering, close communication and regular check-ins between the shop and designer are required to achieve the desired looks.

A costume sketch

Around the time of the first rehearsal, the performers will be scheduled for the first of several sessions with the costume shop. During the first meeting, their tailoring measurements are taken and recorded for use by the shop. At this point performers may also be asked not to cut their hair or to begin to grow facial hair for the style of the show. The performers are asked back a few times during the rehearsal period for **fittings** when their wardrobe is test fit on them for both look and movement considerations. Fittings also give the actor insight to the clothing of their character. This can help them incorporate that visual sensibility into their characters. During the rehearsal process, actors wear **rehearsal clothes** to help them adjust to the wardrobe style of the eventual costume. Actors may be asked to supply some basic rehearsal clothes options like a long skirt or flat shoes for women, or trousers or hard-soled shoes for men. If a period requires something unusual such as hoop skirts or dress swords, the costume shop will supply rehearsal-friendly approximations of those styles. Period wardrobe can seem uncomfortable or ill-fitting at first. In rehearsal, actors need to get used to how high a waistband sits or how tight a bodice is laced to be able to move naturally in character. Along with rehearsal clothes, common personal accessories can be requested from the costume shop for rehearsals. Items such as fans, wallets, purses, compacts, jewelry, and pocket or wristwatches are commonly requested.

Show wardrobe must often allow performers to change quickly between scenes. Clothing is often **rigged** to go on and off quickly. Ample use of Velcro, snaps, and magnets along with replacing shoelaces with elastic, underdressing (wearing something underneath for a quick reveal), and having a helpful dressing crew backstage can make a quick change easier. Often wardrobe purchased off the rack has to be altered or rigged for production use.

Costume shops need a variety of skills to operate. Some shows require bringing in a specialist to handle particular elements of a design. Costume specialties include dyers, wig stylists, leather workers, and costume craft specialists. Costume crafts include jewelry-making, lace tatting, cobbling, millenary, and armor. Millenary arts include all hat making and haberdashery. Armor is common to the theatre, and costume crafts strive to make believable armor from lightweight materials while allowing actors to move comfortably. Painted rubber sheeting and moldable thermoplastics are often used to replicate the look of metallic armor.

The standard tools of a costume shop should seem familiar to most of us, though some of the tools may be industrial or professional versions of the home variety we are familiar with. Sewing machines, large worktables for laying out cloth, and patterns are standard as are irons and ironing boards, steamers, and a laundry area. Spools of thread and cloth bolts in many colors along with drawers of **notions** including buttons and snaps, zippers and trims are found in costume shops, but you will also find less familiar toolds such as a large dye vat or an over-lock serger machine. All the standard equipment in a costume shop is employed to created fabric based elements.

Consider This

Equipment functions best when used only on the materials for which it is intended. Please do not borrow fabric shears from the costume area for cutting non-fabric items.

Earlier it was mentioned that the use of a backstage dressing crew can be very helpful in managing quick changes. A dresser might also be assigned to a particular performer to assist in their costume and makeup application preparations. In the professional theatre union, actors are only required to report to the theatre at "half-hour," that is 30 minutes prior to the scheduled start time of the performance. Though many come earlier to prepare, in this relatively short period of time, a performer may require wardrobe assistance. The relationship between dressers and actors is an important one and is worthy of the time invested in making it work. The performers are literally exposed during these exchanges and are trying to maintain focus for their performances. Meanwhile, the dressers are under the pressure of time and care for details. Both the actor's and dresser's perspectives need to be respected and preserved. Rehearsal and repetition can be key to an organized, efficient, and fast change.

The costume shop maintains all costumes during the performance run. Some items may be laundered, some may be dry cleaned, and some may only be able to be spot cleaned due to their materials or construction. Actors are typically asked to provide their own undergarments and are usually responsible for cleaning them. This leaves the costume staff to focus on any needed repairs and maintaining the look of the show. Laundry may be done daily or less frequently depending on the staffing. Performers take some responsibility for maintaining their costumes by ensuring they are cared for and properly hung and organized, and reporting any maintenance problems. An actor who has left their costumes rumpled up on the stage floor after the last performance should not be too surprised when they find them wrinkled or unwashed for the next show. There is usually quite a bit of wardrobe to coordinate and track, so all parties need to do their best to keep things in order.

Sometimes a play calls for clothing to take some unusual punishments. Blood effects are pretty common. A spill of wine or other food also occurs in a number of plays. The costume shop works with the props designer to come up with solutions that are believable approximations for the audience, but that can also be washed out of the affected wardrobe. Fortunately these effects are often looking for high contrast color impact, and though it might seem like white would be the easiest color to be permanently stained, bleach and other laundry agents can help us get back to white with relative ease. The costume shop should also test other liquids the actors may handle, such as colored waters for drinks. In general natural colorings and liquids without sugars tend to be easier to wash out.

For Further Exploration

Cunningham, Rebecca. 1993. *The Magic Garment: Principles of Costume Design*. Prospect Heights: Waveland Pr Inc.

"National Costumers Association." n.d. Accessed August 16, 2018. https://www.costumers.org/.

MODULE 11

Lighting Design

Most modern theatre spaces are capable of getting quite dark when the lights are turned out. These spaces rarely have windows and when they do, they are usually heavily draped to effectively block out any outside light. Once it is dark, anything the audience sees is visible because of the work of the lighting designer. Theatrical lighting designers are masters of the unique and controlled skill of "painting" with light. As with the other designers, their art is that of a storyteller, and the choices they make for a production support the story being told. Lighting design not only provides **illumination** so we can see the performance, but also utilizes the remaining **functions of light** to create **mood**, **modeling** of the playing area, and to provide a **selective focus** so audiences know where to look in order to follow the story. Light designers manipulate the **controllable qualities of light** at their disposal—**direction** (distribution), **intensity**, **color**, and **movement**—to create their design.

Most plays are set in interiors, though epic plays and musical theatre productions are more likely to have both indoor and outdoor locations. In either case, the lighting designer recreates some version of a lighting situation that the audience is familiar with. We know what the light looks like at sunset on the beach or inside a cozy cabin bathed in firelight, and so we have an expectation of what that should look like on the stage. Therefore, part of a designer's consideration has to be an awareness of that expectation, regardless of whether they choose to support it or take the audience in a different direction.

 A script provides the designer with information regarding place and time period, including specifics regarding years, seasons, and times of day for each scene of the play. All these elements are taken into consideration in the design. The set design, architecture of the theatre space, and the lighting positions it provides, also heavily influence the design of the lighting.

We are used to gauging light largely in terms of sunlight. Even our interiors are often partly illuminated by natural light from windows or skylights. The sun, as we know, is a very bright light source. It produces an even and consistent light over large areas. Creating a reasonable imitation of these qualities is a tall order for the lighting designer. Lighting designers are highly aware of how natural light behaves and develop methods for representing that light with their equipment. A lighting angle of about 45 degrees above the performer produces a light that best approximates daylight from the sun and creates minimum shadows across facial features, allowing the audience to easily read the expressions of the actors.

If two lights are used at that natural 45 degree angle above the performer, but also at an angle 45 degrees out from the performer, the designer can sculpt the contours of that performer by individually adjusting the intensity of the two sources. The brighter source becomes the **key light** and is the motivated source, meaning it is replicating the hypothetical light source of the scene—the sun, a window, or fireplace, etc. The less intense, non-motivated side is the **fill light** and represents the reflected light in the environment. By filtering these two lights additional sculpting of color play becomes possible.

Therefore, many schools of thought about how best to sculpt a playing space within lighting design. The choice of angles and the distribution of light in the playing area are central to the development of the lighting design.

There are four controllable qualities of light.

Intensity: Relative brightness of lights.

Color: The color created by filters or combination of filtered lights.

Movement: Physical movement of lighting sources and movement created by cued changes in lighting states.

Direction: Angle of lighting source to its target.

There are four functions of light:

Mood: Setting an emotional tone for a scene through use of color, angle, and intensity of light.

Illumination: Providing light by which the audience can see the performance.

Modeling: The use of highlight and shadow to reveal the form of the actors and the stage environment.

Selective focus: Using contrast within the lighting of the stage to create a point of focus for the audience.

Eventually the lighting design is represented graphically as a **light plot** and its accompanying spreadsheet paperwork. The light plot is a **plan** that shows the lighting positions on and above the stage area. Each lighting instrument on the design is drawn to scale on the plan with labels for its purpose, color filter, accessory needs, and desired control channel. The plot is often accompanied by a centerline section, which shows the height of each lighting position. All light plots should include a legend box that serves as a key to the symbols used on the plot. This plot is delivered to the master electrician who ensures all the necessary cables, connectors, color filters, templates, pipes, and anything else needed to install the plot are acquired and delivered to the theatre for the **load-in**. A busy time in the theatre space, the load-in must be carefully planned to efficiently get the equipment installed and working on schedule. Once the lighting plot has been installed and tested and the scenery has been installed for the production, the **focus call** can begin. During the focus call, a crew of electricians, led by the master electrician, turns on each instrument on the plot, one by one, and guided by the lighting designer, set its position and physical attributes for the show. This process is further complicated because it involves lifts and ladders that must be moved around scenic items and the theatre architecture in order to reach the lights and move them into position. Once the lights have all been focused to the designer's specifications, the work of setting and recording individual cues for the show can begin.

There's More to Know

Theatre instruments are hung on pipe battens that have electrical circuits attached to them or onto pipe battens that are rigged to carry heavy weight loads. The lights themselves clamp onto the pipes via a "C-clamp." The C-clamp wraps around the pipe to allow the light to be tightened in place without the danger of slipping off. Still, theatrical lights hung overhead should also be equipped with a safety cable that serves as a fall-arrest so even if the C-clamp fails, the safety cable wrapped though the yoke of the instrument and around the batten will prevent the instrument from falling to the ground.

To hang an instrument, first hook the open C-clamp over the batten or pipe and hand tighten its bolt. Once the bolt is snug, the light cannot fall from the pipe. You can now connect the safety cable over the pipe ensuring that it is run through the yoke of the instrument. Next, use a wrench to tighten the C-clamp bolt to the pipe, then orient the fixture towards its eventual focus position. Ensure that it is right side up and all of its bolts are snug. If you are using a shuttered instrument, pull out all shutters to open the instrument. Finally, connect the instrument to a dimmer circuit and to any control cables as needed. Some designers prefer to have the color filters installed when the instruments are hung, others prefer to place them during focus.

Reverse this procedure to strike the instrument.

A **cue** for lighting can be thought of as a snapshot or a single moment when a group of lights are set at various **intensities** to achieve the desired look for that on stage. The snapshot is recorded into a **lighting control console** (essentially a specialized computer), and then the next snapshot of a look of the next moment is recorded. The lighting console is then able to play back each snapshot in order and with a preset time to fade between the looks. The action of fading between two snapshot looks provides the audience a sense of movement of light as some lights fade out in one area, while others come up on another part of the stage. In this way, the lighting designer tells the audience where to look. As humans, we always look to the point of highest contrast in our field of vision, so the designer guides the audience members' eyes to the point of focus and details of the action through the use of lighting contrast. This is one of the ways lighting design helps to tell a story. Cues can also help the audience to know when scenes begin and end though the use of **blackouts**. Scene shifts may occur in a **shift light** that helps the audience to distinguish them from the central action of the play. **Bump-up** or **bump-out** cues may be used for emphasis or to signal the audience to applaud a specific moment. Designers are careful to ensure the rhythm of the lighting cues matches the natural rhythm of the unfolding story.

The designer creates moods through the manipulation of color and intensity of lights, broadcasting from a variety of angles and directions. The way a designer models the light on the performers and scenic environments with these various light sources is akin to painting the stage with light. The use of highlight and shadow allows for lighting changes from subtle to extreme. Lighting is an art that requires a great deal of calculation and equipment management to get a plot in the air and the artful manipulation of these elements to create the visuals the audience experiences.

There are five common lighting directions and angles.

Front light: Directional light coming directly towards the actors' front as they face the audience. This light is of primary importance as it allows the audience to read the actors expressions. It can flatten the visual so performers look 2-D unless supplemented by other lighting angles.

Backlight/rim light: Directional light from behind an actor that creates a rim of light allowing them to be visually separated from backgrounds and giving them dimensionality.

Sidelight: Directional light hitting an actor from the side. This angle provides definition of shape and a sharp outline. Can be used to enhance theatricality.

Sidelight angles for dance lighting:

High sidelight: High, overheard light often hung from electrics over the stage.

Head/shoulder light: A sidelight at approximately 5-6 feet high.

Mid/waist light: A sidelight at approximately 3-4 feet high.

Shin light: A sidelight at approximately 1-2 feet high.

Top light/down light: Directional light from above an actor. Can provide a sense of isolation, but causes shadows from the nose and brow.

Up light: An unusual directional light. Can recall a sense of Vaudeville footlights.

The lighting instruments fall into several basic categories. Theatrical lighting instruments, or luminaires, are either **hard-edged lights** or **soft-edged lights**. When we think of a spotlight, we usually think of a **follow-spot**, or one that follows a performer across the stage, keeping them in the center of a bright circle of light. The clear distinction of the edge of this circle of light is what we refer to as a "hard-edged light." We can see where it stops. Often we are interested in isolating a performer from the area around them and need the definition of a sharply defined edge to show the audience this moment of separation. A soft-edged light doesn't have this clearly distinct edge, but instead has a faded edge, making it harder to discern where its light actually stops. Modern hard-edged fixtures use a lens or system of lenses to create the even field of light they produce. The adjustment of those lenses can soften their hard edges to become less discernible. This allows a designer to use a series of hard-edged instruments together by softening their edges until they blend into a large field of light.

The most common types of theatrical instruments are discussed in Module 12, Lighting Equipment and Control Systems.

For Further Exploration

Essig, Linda, and Jennifer Setlow. 2012. *Lighting and the Design Idea*. Boston: Cengage Learning.

"Stage Lighting Textbook." n.d. Accessed August 16, 2018. https://www.stagelightingtextbook.com/.

Lighting Equipment and Control Systems

Here is a list of the most common fixtures, or luminaires, in use today.

Hard-edged or profile fixtures: These fixtures produce a sharply defined beam of light.

Ellipsoidal reflector spotlights (Also referred to as ERS or Leko): These hard-edged fixtures are the traditional workhorses of theatrical lighting. They produce a narrow beam of light that can be effectively transmitted over long distances. The older units use a two-lens system and an elliptically shaped **reflector** to collect and concentrate the light. The reflector captures all the light emitted by the **lamp** and reflects it toward the two lenses. The first of these two **plano-convex lenses** (flat-planed on one side and convex on the other) gathers the light from its flat surface and concentrates (refracts) it toward its center as the beam passes through the convex shape of the lens. The second lens takes the now concentrated light and spreads it out over the flat surface as it leaves the fixture. Between the two lenses where the light has been concentrated, a set of **shutters**, a series of flat metal flags, can be used to block or limit a beam of light. This allows the light to be shaped and prevents objects that should not be seen from being illuminated. The slot between lenses also allows us to insert a **template** image. A template is a cut-out image through which the light passes to project that image over an area or surface. Templates, also known as **go-bos**, come is an infinite variety of shapes, and modern gobos can either be a laser cut metal plate or a full-color image printed on glass. A template can be used to create texture in light or to project a graphic image. As the light passing through two lenses, the image turns both upside down and backwards, so the shutters operate on the opposite side of the instrument from the projected light. Also, the template pattern needs to be inserted both upside down and backwards in order to project correctly.

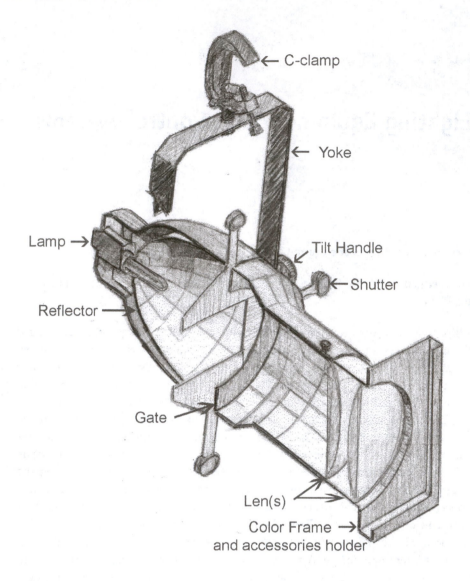

C-clamp

Yoke

Lamp →

Tilt Handle

Shutter

Reflector

Gate

Len(s)

Color Frame →
and accessories holder

An axial style ellipsoidal reflector spotlight

Ellipsoidal reflector spotlights have been around for many years, and theatres may have an inventory of older units. They may be mounted axially, when the lamp enters directly through the rear of the reflector, and radially, when the lamp enters the reflector at a downward angle. Recent advances in these fixtures have made them more efficienct and given them greater clarity. Better design, improved materials for the reflectors and lenses, more efficient lamps, and improvements in the user interface (the ability to move or "zoom" the lens or lenses), have vastly improved the latest fixtures. Most ellipsoidal reflector spotlights are still incandescent lamps of high wattage, though LED fixtures are improving in this market and will eventually become common.

When using an ERS, it is important for designers to consider both the instruments **beam angle** and its **field angle**. The beam angle refers to the area within the cone of light where the strength of the beam is no less than 50% of the brightest area it produces. The filed angle is the outer ring of the cone wherein the brightness dips below 50%. Designers often plot equipment so field angles overlap between instruments to make up for the brightness lost at the edges of the beams.

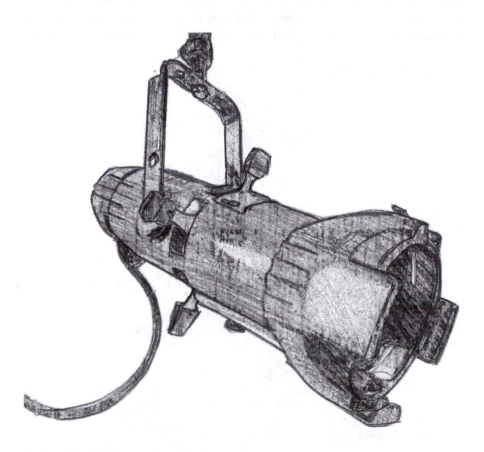

A modern ellipsoidal fixture

Soft-edged or wash fixtures: These fixtures produce a diffused light.

Fresnel: A Fresnel can be recognized by the concentric circular pattern on its lens. This "step lens" is similar to the plano-convex lens, but rather than a thick convex face, the shape has been cut-away to create steps that maintain the curve without the thickness. The back of the lens is textured to further diffuse the source. This lens was originally invented for use in lighthouses. They produce a relatively even field of soft light. A Fresnel is equipped with an adjustable track that allows the lamp source and reflector to be moved closer to and away from the lens, thereby changing the size of the projected cone of light from **spot** to **flood**. Though these fixtures do not have the ability to use shutters to shape their light output, adding a **barn door** to the instrument allows the flaps of the barn door to block the light as it leaves the fixture.

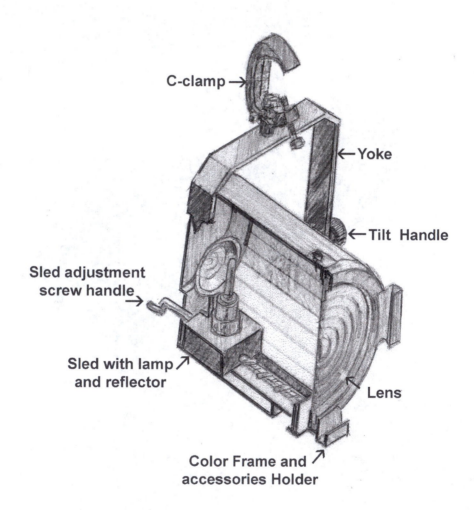

A cut-away view of a Fresnel

Parabolic aluminized reflector (PAR): A PAR light uses a parabolic shaped reflector to capture the source light and redirect it toward the stage. The instrument itself is merely a housing for the lamp and reflector, which come as one solid unit much like a headlight from a car. PAR cans, as they are commonly known, produce a light shape that is elliptical rather than round. Lamps are available with varying widths of spread from vary narrow to narrows to medium and wide spreads. A workhorse of rock tours, these lights are durable and very quick to focus as only the angle of the fixture and the position of the lamp inside it must be adjusted. PAR lamps are sized by measuring in 1/8" segments across the glass face. Sizes range from a PAR16, which is 2" across to PAR64, which is 8" across.

A PAR64

Striplight or **borderlight:** These units are long multi-lamp fixtures made to create a smooth wash of light for backdrops and cycloramas. Most often manufactured in three- or four-circuit styles, they allow for a pre-spaced series of cells to work together to create an even field of colored light projected onto a backdrop or stage area. These incandescent fixtures are now being replaced by LED versions that are more economical, heat-free, and capable of mixing an infinite variety of colors.

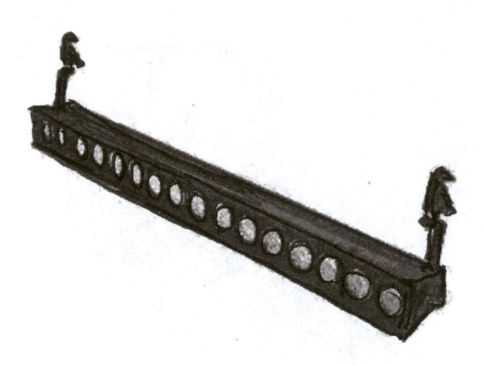

A striplight unit

Cyc. light (**Cyclorama light**): These soft-edged fixtures are meant to light a very large area. They are calibrated to cast their light evenly across a field and hung close to the top of the projection plane. Their asymmetrical reflectors are engineered to cast more of their light toward the bottom of that vertical plane to keep the field more even. These units can be single-cell or multi-cell lights. Like strip lights, cyc. lights are also moving to LED technology for advanced color control.

A multi-cell cyc. light

Incandescent cyc. lights are connected through electrical cables to a **dimmer** unit that allows the electrical flow to their lamps to be reduced so the lights can be dimmed much like the dimmers on your household lights. Theatrical dimmers carry larger loads of current. Most of today's theatrical dimmers are SCR (silicon control rectifier) units and, on average, control about 2,400 watts per dimmer (often abbreviated as 2.4K), although wattage varies, and each unit should be checked for its capacity. Each dimmer has an address much like a street address, that the control console uses to control the voltage the dimmer sends to each fixture. In some theatres, the dimmers are located backstage or in the basement, and miles of cables run out from there to all of the lighting positions of the theatre. In this type of configuration, the cables from the dimmers that appear on the electrics and through raceways to other positions end in numbered **circuits** to which the instruments are connected. These theatres usually also employ a **patch panel**. The patch panel allows for an interface wherein the dimmers and circuits can be connected in any configuration necessary so long as the dimmer's capacity is not exceeded. Some modern theatres are wired as **dimmer per circuit**, meaning no patch panel is necessary as each circuit is permanently connected to its own dimmer. Still another dimmer system hangs small dimmer units directly on the electrics and connects them to their power feed cables at those locations. The advantage to a central bank of dimmers is that the dimmers can be noisy while operating and the central bank can be located away from the stage area where the noise will not disrupt the production.

A number of styles and sizes of electrical connectors are common to the theatre. If your show is loading in to a theatre and your equipment is meant to connect with that owned by the theatre, you need to know what style of connectors they use. If the two styles do not match, adapter cables are required to mate the equipment. These adaptors are generally available to rent when needed. Common connectors include **twist-lock**, **stage-pin**, and **standard grounded Edison (PBG) connectors**.

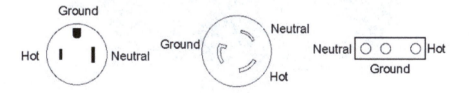

Edison connector, Twist-lock connector, and Stage pin connector

The dimmers are controlled by an electronic signal sent to each individual dimmer address from the lighting control console. A low-voltage electronic protocol language is used to achieve this communication. The **DMX512** (digital multiplexing for 512 channels) signal can simultaneously control 512 separate addresses.

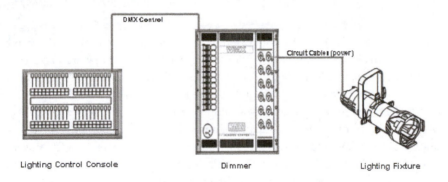

DMX Control

Circuit Cables (power)

Lighting Control Console   Dimmer   Lighting Fixture

Lighting system path

The lighting control board uses **control channels** to interface with the operator. These channels can be arbitrarily connected to the dimmer addresses (soft-patching), so the interface at the board remains flexible. This is important because it allows the designer to organize the hundreds of control channels into a logical system, making it easier to find the channels for the individual instruments or attributes they are trying to control.

A lighting control console

LED fixtures

LED fixtures do not need to be connected to a dimmer because their diodes can be dimmed internally. Therefore, less equipment is needed when they are used. However, modern fixtures, including LED fixtures, do have a variety of functions or attributes that can be controlled remotely by the lighting control console. Each function typically requires a separate DMX address from the board, so a single fixture could consume as many as 20 control channels. If you run above the 512 allowed channels in your DMX communication, you need to add a second DMX universe, which adds an additional 512 control channels. It is not unusual for large shows to run two or three DMX universes, though the lighting control console must be capable of controlling multiple universes.

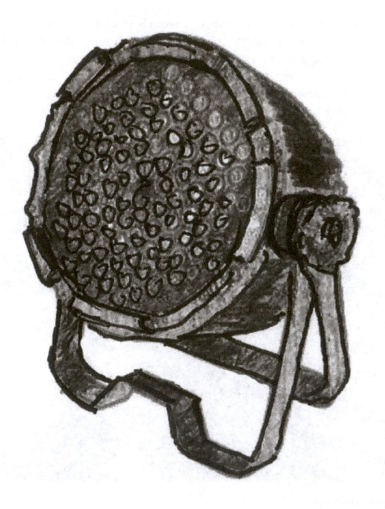

An LED Fixture

There's More to Know

Modern lighting control consoles are designed to allow a programmer working with smart lighting equipment, such as moving lights or LED color controlled equipment, to interface with the attributes of that equipment, like panning, tilting, or color changing graphically rather than by entering the information as % in individual DMX control addresses. This allows for more intuitive programming of these multiple addressed fixtures. Many consoles recognize these smart fixtures once they are connected via DMX or may offer lists of fixture choices to assign to the console's attribute controls. Once assigned, all multiple functions of the devices can be programmed from a single graphic interface. This makes the use of multiple LED fixtures and moving light units far simpler for the programmer who otherwise would have to track each change of range for every control channel the fixtures employ.

Moving light units and **moving mirror units**

Some fixtures are automated and have the ability to rotate, pan/tilt, change color, change size, utilize multiple templates, and strobe. Most moving lights achieve these functions by utilizing a series of motors that move the elements of the fixture. Moving mirror lights motorize only a single mirror onto which the instrument's beam is focused, allowing the light to be reflected around the stage.

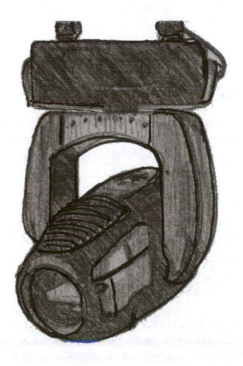

A moving light

A moving mirror light

Safety for a stage electrician

Keeping safe in this environment of temporary installations requires knowledge of the equipment and its limitations and a significant amount of personal focus and discipline. Safety involves using the correct electrical connections, but there are also lifts and ladders that are used to access the equipment.

Ladders must be in good repair and must only be used where all of the ladder's feet can be placed solidly on a sturdy surface. Freestanding, portable ladders are equipped with a "step" at the top, however that step is not intended for standing. The center of gravity of the individual working on the ladder should not be placed above the ladder's recommended working height (typically listed on the ladder itself). A good rule of thumb is that your waist should not be above the top step of the ladder.

Powered lifts must be used in accordance with their safety guidelines, and outrigger supports should always be employed where possible. Electricians should empty their pockets of anything that might fall on workers below, and wrenches or other tools should be secured to the user with a fall arrest.

Keeping all electrical cables in good working order is also key to electrical safety as exposed wires can be a danger. Do not pull on electrical cables or allow the plug to carry the cable's weight. Connection points should be supported with tie line where appropriate. Never touch exposed wires while they are connected to a power source. Power services, dimmers, and cables all have power limitations that must be considered. If you have ever touched a power cable at home and found that it feels hot, that is a sign you are pulling more power through the cord than it is rated for and have a potentially dangerous situation. When more power is pulled through a cable than it is rated to carry, the cable overheats and may melt through its jacket causing an electrical short and possible fire. A cable rated to carry a larger electrical load may be all that is required to correct the problem.

There's More to Know

In order to calculate the electrical load carried by an instrument we need to understand some basics of electricity.

In the United States the electricity in our homes and businesses comes to us as alternating current and is typically sent to us at 115 volts. Our cell phones and other devices that run on batteries are fed by direct current and may be of any number of voltages. In either case, a set of formulas allows us to calculate the factors that govern safe use of the electricity. Volts represent a scale of the relative strength of the flow of electricity (from the supplier). Watts represent the amount of electricity needed to do the work (consumed). Amperage (amps) represents the speed and amount of electricity that can be safely transported.

If we know two of these three figures, we can calculate the third using these formulas: Wattage = voltage x amperage. Amperage = wattage / by volts.

Using the first of these formulas we can tell that if we have a circuit rated at 15 amps (perhaps this is the rating of the breaker for this electrical service), we can calculate the wattage by multiplying the standard 115 volts by the allowable 15 amps to get 1,725 watts. This means we can safely connect lamps that add up to that voltage. This load could be three instruments with 575-watt lamps, two instruments with 750-watt lamps, or 17 instruments with 100-watt lamps.

If we want to power three lighting instruments each equipped with a 575-watt lamp (3 x 575=1,725 watts), we can use the second formula to divide the wattage by the standard 115 volts (1,725/115) to tell us we need a cable rated to carry at least 15 amps to safely transport the electricity. This calculation also tells us that any electrical breakers in the system must be rated for at least 15 amps. Cable is rated by gauge, or thickness of the wire, which is usually printed along the cable's jacket. The gauge of the wire is directly related to the amount of electrical current it can carry safely. Electric current is measured in amps. A cable of made of 14-gauge wire can safely carry 15 amps of electric current.

Calculating electrical loads will keep you and the lighting equipment operating within safe limits.

For Further Exploration

Gillette, J. Michael. 2007. *Theatrical Design and Production: An Introduction to Scene Design and Construction, Lighting, Sound, Costume, and Makeup*. Boston: McGraw-Hill.

"ETC - Theatre, Film, Studio and Architectural Lighting." n.d. Accessed August 16, 2018. http://www.etcconnect.com/.

Sound Design and Equipment

Sound designers are masters of the aural arts. They are responsible for far more than preshow music and doorbells; they decide what music, effects, and vocal microphones are heard and from where. Most modern sound designers are also composers who create the sounds and write the incidental music required for their productions. When commercial recordings are used in productions that will charge for tickets, the producing organization is required to secure the rights to use that music. The high cost of acquiring these rights plus the development of digital recording technology that has put powerful tools for creating and augmenting audio files into the hands of average people has allowed designers to shift from locating appropriate recordings for use to writing original scores. This, coupled with the fact that sound and music can add so much depth to a production, has made sound design a major component of modern theatre.

Sound designers' work falls into several categories. The three main categories are **music**, **reinforcement**, and **effects**. Music may include live musicians as well as recorded music. Music may be a primary element to a scene or may provide an underscore to enhance emotional content. Live musicians require a sound designer to balance the relatively loud sounds of the instruments against the actors and other elements that need to be heard clearly by the audience. In modern musical theatre productions, the orchestra may be in an orchestra pit, another room, or even in another building. Capturing that sound and broadcasting it into an auditorium may become a part of a sound designer's work. Such work bridges into the category of reinforcement, which also includes the sound from actors who wear a microphone during a performance. While microphones are common to musical productions, even some plays performed in larger auditoriums use microphones to pick up the actors voices and broadcast them throughout the theatre space. In this instance, the sound designer strives to have the amplified sound seem as natural as possible to the audience.

The effects category covers any recorded sounds that are played for an audience, including atmospheric sounds, weather sounds, and practical effects. Most theatres are now equipped with a computer program designed to play sounds for live entertainment. These systems allow the cues, volume levels, and routing of the sound to be entered into a playlist-style cue stack. A sound technician can then press a single "Go" button to operate the entire show in sequence. These programs often are also capable of controlling video playback and, in some cases, can be linked to the lighting control console to trigger cues in sequence. Such a program can allow a single technician to run sound, video, and lights from a single cue stack.

Sound designers must also have a deep understanding of their equipment in order to design effectively. All sound systems are composed of the same basic equipment. The sound is routed through this system and processed so it can be delivered to the ears of the audience. The path the sound follows is called the **signal path** or **signal chain**. This chain can be thought of as a series of links that must be connected properly for the chain to be functional. The basic components of a sound system are inputs, the pre-amp, the mixer, signal processor(s), amplifiers, and speakers.

Input or **source** devices are playback devices such as a computer, cell phone, CD player, tape deck, or microphone. If your input source is anything other than a microphone, it is likely that it is sending out an electronic signal at a signal strength known as **line level**. Computers, cell phones, and CD players often have a headphone jack. These jacks operate at this line level signal strength. This signal strength is enough to power the tiny speakers in your earbuds, but if you want to fill the room with sound, you will probably need an amplified speaker because the line level signal does not have enough electrical power to physically push a larger speaker to create the sound waves for you to hear.

Microphones operate on an even lower power signal we call **mic level.** Mic level signals are not even strong enough to power your earbuds because of the way a microphone picks up sounds. A microphone is a device known as a **transducer**. Its job is to capture a physical sound (a pressure wave) and transduce it into an electronic signal. Most microphones operate by using a diaphragm to absorb the pressure waves of live sound. The diaphragm is connected to an electronic or magnetic field, which is affected by the diaphragm's movement in response to the pressure waves. The difference in the affected electronic field is recorded as an electronic waveform (the sound signal) and is then processed and recreated by a speaker (another transducing element) back to a physical pressure wave that our ears can hear. Due to the relatively tiny differences in the electronic field of the microphone, the strength of this interpreted signal is low. Microphone signals must be run-through a **pre-amp** to boost them up to a level that can withstand any electric noise it might be subjected to as it runs through cables and equipment on its way through the signal chain.

Input devices are connected to a mixer and then to signal processing equipment. The **mixer** is key to both routing the signal to the correct devices/outputs and to adjusting input signals for that processing. Processing units include graphic equalizers and effect-based units such as echo and reverb processors, which are devices that alter or augment the signal itself. Most mixers have built in pre-amp functions for mic level signals. Once a signal has been mixed and processed, it is routed to an **amplifier** to further boost its signal power. The signal must be strong enough when it reaches a speaker to not just preserve itself against electronic noise, but to do the work of moving the speakers back and forth to reproduce the physical pressure waves that our ears can hear. The amplifier boosts up the signal to accomplish this work. Speakers are connected directly to the amplifiers, which are where the signal chain ends.

In most theatres this system is already in place, though the sound designer still chooses how it will be operated, the quality of the sound that will be produced, and where the speakers will be located. It is common in modern theatres for speakers to be built in to many locations around the auditorium so that sound is both directional and can be played at lower volumes, which often seems more realistic. The sound designer, in addition to creating the sound recording medium, also creates a plot of speaker locations and how the cables are to be routed to those speakers. It is common for directors to request the use of sound in the rehearsal room prior to technical rehearsals, and so a mini sound system may be required to facilitate that playback.

It is probably not surprising that there are many varieties of all of these devices available for use. A sound designer must be familiar with many pieces of sound equipment to choose what works best for the needs of a given production.

There's More to Know

Microphones come in a variety of styles, and each has its own specialized use.

Dynamic microphone: Durable and inexpensive microphone for voice and instruments.

Omni directional microphone: Usually used in recording studios, these microphones pickup sounds from all directions.

Condenser microphone: A battery powered microphone usually used in recording studios, that is quite delicate and sensitive.

Shotgun microphone: A microphone capable of picking up sounds from some distance.

Wireless hand-held microphone: A hand-held microphone that sends its signal wirelessly to a remote receiver.

Wireless lavaliere/body microphone: A small, pin-on microphone that sends its signal wirelessly to a remote receiver, sometimes taped onto the skin or woven into the hair of a performer.

PZM/PCC microphone: Boundary microphones often placed at the edge of a stage deck to pick up reflected sounds.

In addition to capturing sounds with microphones, sound designers must also provide **monitor** feeds of sound to orchestras and singers so they can keep in tune and time with one another. It may be that an individual performer does not need or want to hear the entire sound scape, but just a part of it. A singer may only need to hear the piano to sing their part and not the drums. In musical theatre, the same performers wearing a wireless body microphone may also wear a wireless in-ear monitor. These devices and their microphone counterparts work essentially like a mini radio station broadcasting from one end and receiving the signal at the other. Because a production may have many of these wireless devices working at one time, they must all be broadcasting on separate frequencies to avoid overlap. The frequencies of these devices are in the same range as those walkie-talkies, police radios, and other public broadcasters operate within. It is imperative that all frequencies are checked for cross-traffic at each venue.

There's More to Know
Stereo vs. monaural (mono) signals:

In a monophonic, or "monaural," system a single channel carries the audio signal. Thus, each speaker in the system receives the same signal information. This can help provide clarity in large systems with many speakers. Stereo, or stereophonic, systems send two independent audio channels played through two speakers (or sets of speakers). This allows the system to reproduce an image of sound in the room by manipulating the specific level and phase of each signal.

Every theatre space has its own natural sound. Some have an obvious echo, or a slap-back effect that doubles voices. Some are warm sounding and perfect for the unamplified voice. Others are better for music and muddy voices. Many of the acoustical properties of any room are created by the room's architecture and the soft and hard surfaces the sound encounters. The pressure waves that create sound are easily bounced off hard surfaces and absorbed by softer surfaces. It is common for sound levels to be set for a production in an empty auditorium during technical rehearsals and then found to be too soft when the theatre fills up with bodies that not only absorb sound, but also make quite a bit of noise themselves, even just by breathing and shifting in their seats. Sound designers must listen to each room they work in to overcome its particular acoustical difficulties.

No matter what equipment makes up the sound system, a series of devices need to be interconnected to complete the **signal path**. A series of sound specific cables connect the devices. Sound cable falls into two major categories: balanced and unbalanced. As we have learned, we must use a stronger signal than a mic level to process that signal through the system to keep electronic noise from affecting its quality. All of our connector cables are running in, around, and through powered devices. Any leaked electrical power can muddy a sound signal, and so using shielded cables in good repair and with tight solid connections can help keep the signal clear. A **signal to noise ratio** is often mentioned when talking about sound routing. You want the strongest signal with the least noise possible. When it comes to connecting cables, a **balanced cable** will do a better job of keeping out electronic noise than an **unbalanced cable**. The difference between the two is easy to detect. A balanced cable has three wires to transport the signal, while an unbalanced cable has only two. In an unbalanced cable, one wire carries part of the electronic signal and also doubles as the shielding for the core wire. The shielding wire's job is to channel any electronic noise away from the wire carrying the sound signal. A balanced cable sends the signal out on two wires; one of them carries a signal that has its phase inverted. This allows for the two signals running parallel to one another to directly cancel each other's potential to leak, resulting in less signal interference. The third wire is then free to shield the signal wires and ground out electronic interference. It makes sense to always use a balanced cable when you can to help protect your signal.

Consider This

Feedback is that nasty ear-splitting sound that can come out of a system when microphones are in use. A loop can be created when a microphone is in the path of the sound broadcast from the speakers. The microphone then picks up its own sound, which is then amplified again by the system, and which it then picks up again from the speaker. This loop continues growing louder until the input or the system volume is turned down. Nobody enjoys hearing feedback, but the immediate solution is simple: turn it down!

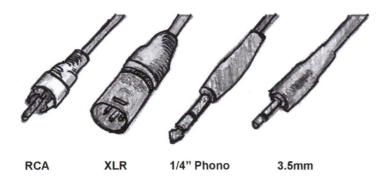

| RCA | XLR | 1/4" Phono | 3.5mm |

Common connectors

Balanced = XLR and ¼" if TRS (tip, ring, sleeve)
Unbalanced = ¼" if TS (tip, sleeve), RCA, and common 3.5mm "mini jack"

The speaker wires that connect speakers to amplifiers are not balanced cables due to the high strength of the electronic signal they carry, so they can still be affected by ambient electrical noise. Care should be taken to ensure that these cables are never routed alongside power extension cords or lighting cables, which can result in a buzz in the speakers. If the cables must cross, make sure they cross each other at a 90-degree angle and do not run along each other's length.

For Further Exploration

Gillette, J. Michael. 2007. *Theatrical Design and Production: An Introduction to Scene Design and Construction, Lighting, Sound, Costume, and Makeup*. Boston: McGraw-Hill.

Rossing, Thomas D., F. Richard Moore, and Paul A. Wheeler. 2001. *The Science of Sound, 3rd Edition*. San Francisco: Pearson.

"Association of Sound Designers " n.d. Accessed August 16, 2018. http://associationofsounddesigners.com/.

Scene Painting and Color Theory

It could be said that illusion is central to theatrical production and, therefore, something designers try to create. Scenic painting is the artful application of paint to create visual illusions on the surfaces it covers. Whether it is mimicking a material surface such as wood or stone or adding artificial depth to a 2-D surface through painted shadows, scenic painting is the process of creating a visual illusion. The French use the term "trompe d'l'oeil," translated as "fools the eye," to refer to the art of painted illusions. Set designers deliver paint renderings to the scenic artists who execute the designs on a much larger scale. There may be several meetings with the designer and samples may be painted before the exact methods and colors for executing the scenic painting can be established. Common painting methods are described later in this Module, but to appreciate this art we must first have an understanding of some of the basic theories regarding color that rule over the art of theatrical illusions.

Color plays a central role in creating a convincing environment and effectively transporting the audience into the world of the story. Color is found in the sets, the costumes, and the lighting, but the audience's perception of all color is influenced by the lighting. This is happens in part because the choice of color filters on the lights will affect what the audience will be able to reference as "white." We perceive most of the natural world under white light (full-spectrum light), and when we are presented with a situation in which that light is filtered, our perceptions of color are altered. The lighting designer closely controls the audience's perception of color in the sets and costumes by selecting color filters for the lights. The coordination of the lighting these elements is a central concern for the entire creative team.

There's More to Know

How our eyes perceive color:

Our eyes receive light energy waves, and through the excitement the eye's receptors, translate this light energy, which is either emitted by or reflected by an object, into the electrochemical information our brains then interpret for image and color. The light is re-

---

ceived through two groups of nerves in our eyes: rods, which receive faint light waves and help us to see in low-light situations and at night, and cones, which receive higher energy light and respond to the specific wavelengths of red, blue, and green light.

Our sun produces an intensely bright light that is made up of a variety of color wavelengths of light. Combined, these wavelengths fall over our planet as full-spectrum "white light." We have all seen a rainbow, and most of us have experimented with a prism and understand that it is possible to divide white light into its constituent colors. When full-spectrum light hits a colored object, the object absorbs a portion of the light energy. The portions absorbed are the wavelengths that do not resemble the inherent color of the object. The portions of the light energy that are akin to the inherent color of the object are reflected off of the object, and those waves are reflected into our eyes, and onto our rods and cones, which interpret the image. So, if full-spectrum sunlight hits a red playground ball, the red wavelengths of that light are reflected to our eyes, and we see a red ball. The other wavelengths (all other colors) are absorbed by the ball and not reflected. This is also why darker colored objects, like a black car, become hotter when left under the sun. They absorb a lot of light energy that becomes heat energy. If we can only perceive an object's color when the corresponding wavelength of light is available to reflect off its surface, then in an environment where full-spectrum light is not available all color information can be affected. A theatrical lighting designer controls the colors an audience perceives during a show by filtering all of the available light. You have probably noticed that it is difficult to perceive color in relative darkness. When light is limited, our cones cannot receive the levels of energy reflecting off of objects to interpret their color information. Our eyes must instead rely on our rods to interpret the light minus the color information, which makes things look a bit grey.

We have all studied color throughout our entire lives. We learned in art classes how to mix a variety of colors from a few **primary colors**, but much of how we are affected by color may be innate to us. Our associations of color fall into two main categories: **natural associations** and **cultural associations**. Natural associations are those that we are born with and are survival-based associations. Red is a color of warning; a red object may be hot or possibly poisonous, and red is the color of spilled blood. Green is the color of vegetation, our food. Blue is the color of life-giving water. It is beneficial to our survival to recognize the dangers these colors communicate. Other associations are cultural and are based on how we grew up and where we live. In the United States, green may be associated with money, while in other cultures green may be associated with luck or even fertility. Both natural and cultural associations are powerful in affecting all of us. We rely heavily on our visual senses to interpret the world around us, and color is an important factor in that interpretation.

Color terminology

Hue: A color or the qualities that differentiate one color from another.

Saturation (also Chroma): Relative percentage of a hue within a color mixture.

Value: The relative lightness or darkness of a color.

Tint: A high-value color achieved by adding white pigment or light.

Shade: A low-value color achieved by adding several hues or black.

Tone: A medium value color achieved by adding black and white, or by mixing it with its' complimentary hue.

There's More to Know

Color Temperature:

All color has an association with temperature; we regularly refer to cool colors and warm colors. Color temperatures are based on a scientific notion of what temperature a theoretical "black body" would have to be to emit light of a given color. A Kelvin scale provides the units of measure for color temperature. Cool colors like blues are rated at over 5000 K, while warmer colors fall between 2700-3000 K. Photography and videography is greatly affected by the color temperature of the light on their subjects, and theatrical lighting may not always appear as intended when recorded in these mediums. Theatre lighting fixtures generally use tungsten-based filaments, which burn at a fairly low color temperature even before being filtered. When film or video are used to capture theatrical presentations, the temperature of the light may need to be adjusted for the device to capture what our eyes see naturally.

You probably remember from grade school lessons that there are three primary colors: red, blue, and yellow. What you might not have learned is those are the three primary colors for **pigment**, but not for light. There is a separate color wheel that represents how color of light is organized and mixed. The difference between pigment and light is partly due to our eyes and how we, as humans, perceive color though our eyes. We have receptors in our eyes that interpret red, blue, and green light. Our brains use these three colors of light to interpret our visual perceptions of the world.

From art class, we know we can mix two primary pigment colors together to make a new color. Mixing two primary colors will result in a **secondary color**. In pigment mixing the secondary colors are orange, green, and purple. If we combine a secondary color with the primary color that it neighbors on the color wheel, we create a new **tertiary color**. In this system of pigment colors, if we **additively mix** colors together, they become darker as we add hues, and will eventually appear near black as we continue to add colors.

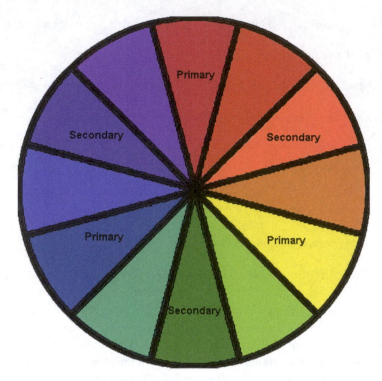

A color wheel for pigment

Light has its own color wheel; its primary colors include green rather than yellow. The color wheel for light is based on the human reception of visual information. Our eyes do not have a specific receptor for yellow, so when we see a yellow object our eyes read the wavelengths of the red and green light, and, in sensing a small amount of each wavelength, our brains interpret the impulse as yellow. While pigments additively mix toward black, a variety of colored lights additively mix toward white as all of the various wavelengths combine to fill in the spectrum to approach a "white" light. Through the use of color filters, lighting designers remove portions of the spectrum from an individual light that would otherwise broadcast a full-spectrum. This is called subtractive coloring. The combination of a number of these individually filtered lights onto an object additively mixes together the available light that will strike that object. If we filter all red light from an environment, then a red object will not appear red to our eyes since no red wavelengths are available to be reflected back to them. If all the light on the red object is a green wavelength, it will appear a dark color that looks grey to black because the green light is a complementary color to the red object. This kind of control over what the audience sees allows a lighting designer to affect all the colors on a stage through their choice of lighting filters.

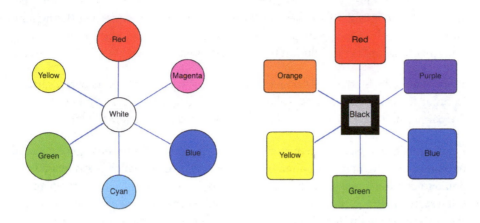

Color wheel for light (left) & color wheel for pigment (right)

Lighting filters (gels)

As we have learned, theatrical lighting instruments emit a full-spectrum, white light. Designers then use a color filters, or gels, to limit parts of the spectrum projected from the light. These filters are thin colored sheets of translucent polycarbonate or polyester that are placed in front of the light source. Only the part of the spectrum of light that is akin to the color of the filter is allowed through. All other parts of the spectrum are absorbed by the filter, resulting in the projection of a limited wavelength of light. Because all other wavelengths are absorbed (as heat) darker filters do not last as long as lighter filters and may melt or fade with time. The relative strength of a light is greatly affected by how much energy is transmitted through a given filter. **Transmission** is the term that describes the percentage of source light that passes through a given filter. Sample decks of colored filter swatches are available from manufactures and generally list the percentages of transmission for each color filter. A darker color filter may have a transmission of only 10-20%. Color filters are used individually in an instrument because stacking two filters only serves to diminish the amount of light that passes through the filters since each individual filter removes all wavelengths of light other than those akin to it. Lighting designers use the color wheel of light to develop a color palette that will color the production's world as intended. A designer creates a look specific to the production by picking three or more filter colors in a triad configuration on the color wheel, putting them on three separate lights, and blending them together in a single projection area where they combine to create the show's "reference white." The use of just two **complementary color** filters (those directly opposite on a color wheel) can appear to mix toward white since their opposition on the color wheel allows greater coverage of the apparent spectrum. As theatre fixtures are quite bright and can feel harsh, a mixed white light will always appear richer and more vibrant to an audience than using unfiltered full-spectrum, white light.

Scenic painting often takes advantage of the filtered spectrum of the lighting designer's palette in order to achieve its illusionary effects. Knowing that the lighting allows some colors to appear prominent and some to recede, the painter chooses hues that best support the illusion their paint is intended to create.

Scenic paint effects are largely achieved through the layering of colors over a surface. In order to achieve layering that allows the previously laid layers to show through, the painter must use a series of thinned paint **washes** to complete the effect.

Paint is made up of several elements. The color of paint is due to the **pigment** added to its mixture. Pigment is an often dry, colored particulate, which is suspended in a liquid to give the liquid hue. The liquid itself has two purposes: it allows the pigment to be spread over a surface and includes glue that permanently binds the pigment to the surface. The paint liquid is part **vehicle**, which allows the paint to spread and is eventually evaporated or absorbed, and part **binder,** which is the glue that adheres the particles of pigment. A forth component that is common to house paints is **filler**, which is particulate matter that increases the opacity of the paint for better coverage.

When creating washes by thinning paints (adding more of the vehicle component), a scenic artist has to be careful not to thin so much that the binder can no longer effectively glue the pigment to the surface, or the paint will easily rub off onto costumes and actors.

Though it is common for modern theatres to work primarily with water-based latex paints, it is possible to encounter other types of paint and solvents in a scenic paint shop. Always read labels on the products you are working with. Shops are required to keep a binder of SDS (safety data sheets) for all chemical compounds they stock. These sheets serve as guides for safe use, personal protection requirements, and cleanup of chemical products.

Most commonly, scenic artists are asked to replicate the textures of materials such as woods or stone onto scenery, though creating visual depth through manipulation of highlight and shadow is also central to the art. As temporary constructions, sets are often built of relatively light and inexpensive materials, though often they represent rather ornate interiors. So scenic artists paint wood to look like more expensive wood or wood to look like stone or metal. Scenic artists are masters of these illusions and create most of them through the use of relatively few application techniques. The most common application techniques are scumbling, dry-brushing, spattering, sponging, stippling, and rag-rolling. The combination of these application methods produces some amazing painted illusions. Painted light and shadow can add very convincing detail and depth to these illusions, but must be carefully coordinated with the lighting design.

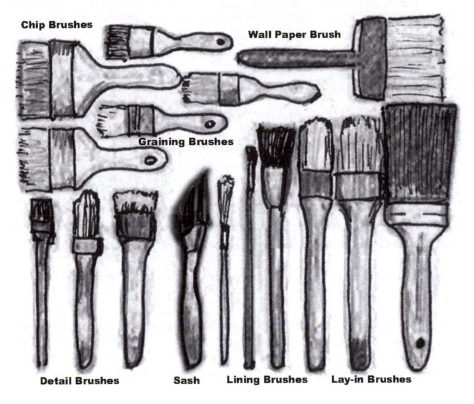

Chip Brushes

Wall Paper Brush

Graining Brushes

Detail Brushes   Sash   Lining Brushes   Lay-in Brushes

A variety of shapes and sizes of paintbrushes

Brushes

There are many different kinds of brushes that are used to paint in a production.

Priming: A wide thick brush for covering large areas quickly.

Lay-in: A flat-tipped brush with a thick ferule of bristles to carry large amounts of paint.

Graining: A brush cut to have void areas for creating random graining.

Liner: A flat edged brush for outlining and details.

Sash: A steeply angled brush for cutting in against window framing.

Chip: A commonly available, inexpensive brush well-suited to dry-brushing technique.

Roller: A round tube capable of rolling paint onto a surface. The nap of the roller indicates the thickness of its cover and will determine the texture the roller is best suited to cover or create.

Paint application techniques

There are many different paint application techniques that can be used sets.

Scumble: To wet-blend two or more colors together using multiple brushes.

Spatter: To spray small dots of paint onto a surface by flicking the paint of the ends of the bristles.

Dry brush: To drag a nearly dry brush across the surface of a base color in order to leave a series of streaks of paint along the surface.

Stipple: Using the blunt ends of the bristles of a brush to stamp color onto a surface to provide visual texture.

Rag roll: Using a length of cloth dipped into paint and wrung out to roll across a painted surface to apply a roving line. Especially useful for marble and stone effects.

Paint layers (coats): Applying multiple layers of paint are applied to a surface

Prime coat: A layer intended to seal the surface of the object and provide a uniform surface for the base coat.

Base coat: The foundational coat for the intended technique, it should match the hue and value of the finished product.

Texture coat: A thick coat of paint, plaster or other medium applied to add a three-dimensional texture to a surface.

Top coat: A final coat, usually clear or lightly tinted, to add a sheen to the finished technique.

Creating a Faux Wood Grain

First observe a sample of the wood you are attempting to replicate. Look at the quality and colors of its grain and the tones of its base colors. Begin with a two-color base coat of the extreme light and dark tones of its base colors scumbled together applied in the direction of the grain. Wood grain can be created either in a wet-blend or a dry technique. To wet-blend colors, the grain colors are brushed into the still wet base scumble. This technique can produce subtle results with enough time and care. Dry techniques work well when covering larger areas and can also be very controlled with practice. To use the dry technique, allow the base scumble to dry completely, then dry brush thin grain colors over the base, letting each color dry between steps. In either method, waiting for the base and grain layers to dry before applying toning glaze and/or top coat for sheen will make for a convincing effect. The toning glaze is often a thinned version of the most prominent grain color sponged over the entire piece to help blend the colors together. It can be mixed into a glaze medium that will also add sheen to the finish or can be covered with a clear top coat for sheen once dry.

Creating a faux wood grain

Creating a Faux Stone Surface

Scumble two or more colors together on the surface to supply variation to your base. Once dry, apply a series of spatter coats to add visual texture to the effect. A tint and a shade of the mid-tone from your base colors can be thinned to spatter consistencies appropriate to the size of spatter dot you are trying to achieve. Thinner paints produce larger spatter dots. If any areas look too bold after spatters are applied, applying a third layer of spatter made from the untinted mid-tone base color can break up the two previous spatters. If your final effect is that of a stone path, paint your mortar lines between stones prior to applying the shade spatter to help blend the surfaces together. Add highlights and shadows along edges of stones to add dimension.

A faux stone surface

To create a convincing sense of depth on a scenic surface, you must work in concert with the lighting designer so all shadows, both painted and those created by scenery and actors, work in the same direction. The direction of the shadows is established by the direction of key light sources of the light plot. Once the direction of the stage lighting has been established, the placement of highlights and shadows can be calculated for the scenic painting.

Light and shadow enhancement

For Further Exploration

M.A, Associate Professor William H. Pinnell B. A. 2008. *Theatrical Scene Painting: A Lesson Guide*. Carbondale: Southern Illinois University Press.

Sherwin, Stephen G. 2006. *Scene Painting Projects for Theatre*. Boston: Focal Press.

"Color Matters." n.d. Accessed August 16, 2018. https://colormatters.com/.

MODULE 15

Stage Crews and Production Etiquette

In order for a theatrical production to run smoothly and efficiently, there must be some sort of hierarchy or reporting structure. The stage crew's organizing force is the stage manager. While crews may receive input on their jobs from designers, directors, and even cast members, they should remember the stage manager is the captain of their ship. The entire company comes together in order to produce an experience for an audience, and, as the stage manager is in charge of interfacing all of the elements of that experience, they must be the one to lead both the process and the people involved in it.

As a member of the stage crew, you may be asked to be on a variety of sub-crews for a production. Your crew may have a head technician who leads your group, such as a head electrician, lead dresser, or master flyperson. If so, you may do most of your reporting through them as they in turn report to the stage manager.

You may be asked to wear a headset for communication during the show. If so, know that many people need to use the same system to conduct the show properly and vocal traffic should always be minimal to keep the lines clear. If you are receiving cues via the headset, you should receive a series of calls for your cue. If you are running a manual or effects board on a production, and there are long stretches of time between cues, you may receive a warning call from the stage manager to tell you that you have a cue coming up soon. The response they require back from you may depend on their own personal needs or on the timing of the other cue traffic, but typically a response of "warned" will suffice to let them know you are ready. The next cue you hear from the stage manager is "stand-by," and the typical response is "standing by." Stand-by cues are given to all operators during a show. The final cue you should receive is a description of the cue or cue number followed by the word "go." The word "go" is the actual directive to take your action at that time. Stage managers will often pause just before the word "go" to place it correctly within the stage action. Once you have finished your action, the stage manager may request that you add a response to let them know your action is "complete."

If you are in a position that only works during scene changes or other specific moments in the show, you may spend quite a bit of time backstage in the dark, waiting for your action. It is tempting sometimes to begin offstage conversations or to become involved with some distraction. However, this should be avoided, as all backstage sounds distract from the onstage action, and can cause you to miss a cue that requires your attention. It is best to remember what we are all there to do our part to support the action of the performance and the audience's experience.

You may be asked to wear all black clothing or "blacks" if you have a backstage job on a show. This allows you to better blend into the masking and to be less visible during blackouts if you need to cross the stage. Be sure your clothing is fully black to blend in well.

Technical rehearsals can be very long and can seem boring. Hours may be spent on short moments in the show. Though your attention is required, bring something to read and a way to keep hydrated. Since rehearsals run long, everyone needs breaks to visit bathrooms and drink water. Make sure the stage manager always knows where you are if you need to leave the room so the rehearsal does not come to a halt due to your absence.

During the run of a production be sure to arrive on time for your call, sign in if there is a sheet setup by the stage manager intended for tracking people, and start checking that everything you handle is in place and working for the show. Your stage manager will develop their own system to check-in with all departments to ensure everything is ready for the performance. Remember that standard production etiquette dictates a shift crew does not enter the stage post-performance to reset or clear the stage until the audience has emptied from the house. This, of course, might be altered if a particularly timely or long cleanup or reset is required.

Theatre is and should be fun. It is a great to become part of a team with a larger goal, but the fun comes from being dedicated to its purpose and to the work it involves. Presenting art is not easy, nor should it be. If it were easy, then there would not be anything special about being really good at it.

Have fun being good!

Glossary

acting area: in lighting; an area of the stage where actors play a moment or scene, and which requires illumination.

acting notes: refinements and corrections given to actors during the rehearsal or performance process. These notes usually come from the director or stage manager.

additive color mixing: in lighting; the combination of several filtered lights on one area. Lighting color mixes toward white light.

amplifier: in sound; a devise that boosts a sound signal to a level strong enough to push a speaker.

arena theatre: a theatre space wherein the audience surrounds the playing area.

apron: the flat extension of the stage that projects from the proscenium toward the audience.

audition: a try-out session in which actors are seen by a director for potential selection to play a role in the show.

balanced cable: for audio; a cable that has three wires to help reduce noise in the signal chain.

barn door: In lighting; an accessory equipped with adjustable flaps to block the source.

batten: pipes suspended above a stage used for supporting scenery, drapery, and lighting.

beam angle: in lighting; the portion of the beam of light that is at least 50% as bright as the center of the beam.

binder: in paint; the glue in the mixture that affixes the pigment to the painted surface.

black box theatre: a theatre space wherein the audience and performance are in one room. These theatres are usually equipped with movable seating to allow for various configurations.

blackout: in lighting; a cue that fades all lights out.

blackout drape: a full-stage, black drape.

blackout traveler: a full-stage, black drape that can open and close horizontally.

blocking: the planned movement of actors around the playing area.

border light: a multi-cell fixture primarily used to light drops. Aka strip light.

breakaway: any prop that has been designed to break apart without injuring the performer.

build schedule: a chart of each piece required for a production with reference to when each stage of construction must be completed.

bump-up: in lighting; a cue that quickly raises the lighting level.

bump-out: in lighting; a cue that quickly goes to a blackout.

butt joint: a simple wood joint in which two pieces are cut square and abutted together.

carriage bolt: a bolt whose upper face has a rounded surface with the underside shaped as a tapered square collar. Used to join wood without leaving a protruding head.

cast: the group of actors playing all the parts in a play.

circuit: in lighting; a numbered cable associated with a diming system.

color: in lighting; one of the four controllable qualities of light, achieved through use of color filters, aka gels.

color rendering: a colored sketch or painting of design elements or costumes.

community theatre: a noncommercial, local group made by and intended for their community.

company: a group including all the members of a theatrical organization or production.

complementary colors: colors opposite from one another on a color wheel.

connector: the style of electrical plug on a piece of equipment.

contact sheet: a document with contact information listed for the entire cast and crew of a production.

control booth: an area or room dedicated to the equipment used to control theatrical equipment for presentation.

consumable: anything that is intentionally used up or destroyed during a production.

control channels: in lighting; the numbers used at the lighting control console to control the actions of the dimmers.

controllable qualities of light: for lighting; intensity, color, movement, direction.

corner block: a thin plywood triangle used to support the corner joints of a flat frame.

costume: the wardrobe and accessories designed for a character in a play.

costume rendering: A designer's full-body sketch of a costume design. Usually colored, often accompanied by fabric swatches.

costume parade: a showing of characters in their wardrobe under stage light for director's approval and adjustments.

counterweight arbor: the vertically tracked weight carriage of a counterweight fly line.

counterweight system: a fly system utilizing a tracked arbor to control the movement of a batten.

creative team: the group of people responsible for the design of a production; typically the director, designers, choreographer, and musical director.

crossover: a method of travelling from one side of the stage to another, unseen by the audience.

cue: a directive for action. For example, a change in lighting.

cue-to-cue: a technical rehearsal in which action around cues is rehearsed but dialogue between is skipped over.

cultural associations: for color; those associations we learn through our culture.

cut drop: a drop that has a profiled edge.

cutter: for costumes; the person who cuts fabric to be sewn into costumes.

cyclorama (aka **cyc**): a large backdrop often used to represent sky. These traditionally wrap around the upstage wings.

cyc light: a lighting fixture designed to light drops and cycloramas.

deck: the stage floor or level built on top of the stage floor.

design presentation: A meeting in which designers present and explain designs to the company.

dimmer: in lighting; a unit that controls the electric supply to the lighting instrument allowing it to fade.

dimmer per circuit: in lighting; a theatre where each lighting circuit is wired to its own dimmer.

direction: in lighting; one of the four controllable qualities of light.

DMX512: in lighting; the electronic protocol language used by control consoles to control lighting equipment.

draper: in costumes; a person who builds wardrobe by draping fabric over a dress form.

draping: the art of building wardrobe by draping fabric over a dress form.

drop: a large flat piece of fabric used as part of the scenery for a show.

dry tech: a technical rehearsal for crews for which the performers are not present.

drywall screws: specialty screws with qualities of sharpness and brittleness.

Edison connector: in lighting; a standard style, two-bladed plug in common use in U.S. homes.

effects: in sound; one of the three major areas of sound design, effects cover any sounds that are not music cues or related to reinforcement.

electric: in lighting, a batten specifically fitted for use as a place to hang lighting instruments.

ellipsoidal reflector spotlight: a standard hard-edged theatrical lighting instrument using a two-lens system and an elliptically shaped reflector.

facing: a surface added to the sides of a platform so that it appears solid.

false proscenium: a portal that sits in front or inside of the natural proscenium creating a new frame for the stage.

field angle: in lighting; the portion of the beam of light that is less than 50% as bright as the center of the beam.

fight call: a preshow rehearsal conducted to review any physical business in a performance to minimize the chance for injuries.

fill light: in lighting; the dimmer or unmotivated source of light representing the reflected light of the scene, it fills the shadows created by the key light.

filler: in paint; particulate matter added to increase its opacity.

first hand: a costume shop employee who assists the costume shop manager in day-to-day operations.

fixed caster: a caster wheel that cannot swivel.

fitting: an appointment for an actor to be fitted into their costume.

flat: theatrical walls built as scenery.

flat-patterning: the use of paper patterns to cut fabric pieces for costumes.

flood: in lighting; to widen the beam of a lighting instrument.

fly: to rig objects in the theatre so they can be lifted and lowered above the stage.

fly system: a system of ropes or cables allowing scenery to be rigged to a grid over the stage.

focus call: a work call to adjust the lighting instruments to the designer's specifications for a production.

follow-spot: a lighting instrument on a rotating base allowing an operator to follow an actor with its beam.

Fresnel: in lighting; a soft-edged instrument with a step lens.

functions of light: in lighting; mood, illumination, modeling, and selective focus.

gel: a common term used to refer to color filters for lights. Gel is a holdover term from days when filters were made of gelatin.

gobo: a common term used to refer to cut-out template patterns for lights.

grand drape: the main curtain on a stage, often richly colored.

grand teaser: a short and wide drape that hangs over the main drape and is often richly colored.

grid: the network of beams above the stage that support the rigging system components.

ground row: a low horizontal scenic element, usually used to hide lighting along the stage floor.

hand: in costumes; the feel of a fabric.

hand prop: a prop handled by performers.

hard-cover flat: a flat frame with a hard face typically ¼" plywood or luaan. Can be flat framed, metal framed, Broadway, or studio style.

hard-edged light: a fixture with a defined edge to its beam of light.

hazer: a unit that continuously puts out a relatively light atmospheric fog.

head block: a multi-sheave block used to change the direction of control lines for a batten.

headset: a part of the communication system used by crews during a performance.

headset system: a communication system allowing crews to remain in contact throughout a theatre.

hex bolt: a bolt fastener with a hexagonal top for easy tightening with a wrench.

hold: a temporary stop of rehearsal action.

house: the audience area of an auditorium.

illumination: in lighting; one of the four controllable qualities of light.

input device: for sound; a playback device or microphone.

intensity: in lighting; relative brightness.

jack: a triangular frame used to brace flats and keep them vertical.

jackknife platform: a platform designed to pivot onstage from a fixed point on one corner.

key light: in lighting; the brighter source of light, motivated by the presumed source of light for the scene.

keystone: a thin plywood brace used to support the rail joints of a flat frame.

lamp: in lighting; the bulb (envelope), base, and filament unit for a lighting instrument.

LED fixture: a lighting fixture that uses light emitting diodes rather than an incandescent source.

leg: a style of drapery, these tall narrow drapes mask the wing space along the sides of a stage.

levels: raised areas on the stage.

lift line: the lines that support a batten in a rigging system.

light plot: a scaled plan showing the placement of lighting equipment for a production.

lighting control console: the interface for control of theatrical lighting. Typically a computer based control that replays preprogrammed lighting cues sequentially.

lighting filters: colored translucent sheets placed in front of lights to filter their spectrum.

lighting rehearsal: a showing of light cues by their designer for the director and stage manager prior to technical rehearsals.

lighting system: the components of lighting equipment that allow for control of lighting states on a stage.

line level: a low-level electronic signal used to route and process sound.

load-in: the time when technical support elements are installed in a theatre for a production.

load-in door: the door or opening provided by a theatre for production equipment to enter the space.

loading dock: an area adjacent to the load-in door where trucks can offload equipment into the space.

loft block: an individual sheave that changes the direction of a line in a rigging system.

main drape: sometimes referred to as a grand drape, the main curtain in a theatre often richly colored.

mask: to hang curtains so they block the audience view of backstage areas.

mic level: a very low-level electronic signal used to transfer the transduced microphone signal into a system for processing. Ordinarily this signal must be run through a pre-amp.

mixer: for sound; a signal routing device allowing adjustment of audio levels from and to various sources.

modeling: in lighting: one of the four functions of light, the use of highlight and shadow to sculpt objects with light.

mood: in lighting; one of the four functions of light, the emotional quality of a lighting moment.

monitor: in sound; a speaker placed so that performers can hear one another.

movement: in lighting; one of the four controllable qualities of light, the physical movement of light sources or perceived movement through changing cues.

moving light: a lighting fixture with motorized components to allow for remote control.

moving mirror light: a lighting fixture equipped with a motorized mirror to allow for remote control of the beam direction.

music: in sound; one of the three primary responsibilities of a sound designer, any music played during a production.

natural associations: for color, any associations we may be born with.

natural stage floor: the top surface of the stage floor without scenery added.

nominal dimension: the dimension of lumber prior to finishing, not the actual dimension.

notions: for costumes; items including buttons, zippers, hooks, and other fabric construction accessories.

orchestra pit: the space between the stage and the auditorium, usually below stage level, where an orchestra can be held.

paper tech: a meeting in which cues are placed in the stage manager's prompt book.

PAR: a lighting instrument using a parabolic reflector lamp.

PARNel: a highbred lighting instrument blending features of a Fresnel and a PAR, producing a soft-edged light.

patch panel: a flexible connection bay where lighting circuits are routed to dimmers.

personal prop: any prop that may be directly associated to a character, may include jewelry, parasols, combs, etc.

pigment: an additive that provides color.

pin connector: in lighting; a three-pin, flat, paddle-style electrical connector., aka stage-pin connector.

pin rail: a horizontal rail where lines are tied off to hold battens at required heights.

places call: a directive made by the stage manager to the company for all to go to the spot they need to be in in order to begin a performance.

plan: a graphic representation drawn as an overhead view.

plano-convex lens: in lighting; a lens that is flat on one side and has a convex curve profile on the other.

platform: a framed unit intended to support people or any raised area on a stage.

playback: the replaying of recorded media or type of media supported by equipment.

playing area: the area of the stage where the audience can view a performer.

portal: an archway formed by two legs and a border or similar framed opening.

practical: an item that must function onstage as it would in real life.

pre-amp: an amplifier designed to boost a mic level signal to a line level.

preproduction: the time before rehearsals and construction have begun.

preview performance: a public performance given before the advertised opening of a production.

primary colors: the base colors from which all others can be mixed. For pigment: red, blue, and yellow. For light: red, blue, and green.

proscenium theatre: a traditional theatre space where the audience and the stage are essentially two rooms with an archway cut from the adjoining wall.

production concept: the creative interpretation of a script that unifies the artistic vision of the creative team.

production meeting: a conference of appropriate production team members to share information and updates.

production resources: assets available to realize a given production.

production schedule: the calendar developed to track a production from inception through performances.

production team: the group of people responsible for realizing a production.

professional: generally refers to those paid for their efforts rather than volunteers.

profile flat: a flat wall with a shaped edge or edges.

prompt book: a copy of the script, maintained by the stage manager, that records the blocking and cues for a production.

property list: a list of all prop elements required for a production.

pull: to choose an item in the theatre stock for production use.

put-in rehearsal: a special rehearsal for an actor taking over an existing role.

raked stage: a stage for which the floor of the playing area has ben raised at the back such that it angles up and away from the audience. This arrangement lends a false depth to the playing area.

reflector: in lighting; the element that collects wasted light from the lamp and refracts it in the direction of the lens.

reinforcement: in sound; one of the three main responsibilities of a sound designer, the balance and amplification of live sound elements and voices.

rehearsal clothes: clothing worn by actors during rehearsal periods to approximate the style of wardrobe they will wear for the show.

rehearsal report: Daily reports sent to the production team by the stage manager that chronicle the events of the previous rehearsal and list needs for upcoming rehearsals.

rehearsal room: the space where the directors and actors develop the performance.

rehearsal prop: an approximation of a show prop given to actors for the rehearsal period.

rehearsal schedule: a schedule of all rehearsals and their locations for a production.

resident designers: staff designers who may be assigned design work within a theatre season.

revolve: a rotating platform or stage.

rigged/rigging: something that has been hung on ropes or cables. In costumes; a garment that has been altered for fast removal.

rise/run: refers to stairs and the relative change in height over each individual tread's depth.

rope set rigging: a flying system relying on a pin rail and sandbags to counter weight placed on a batten.

run: the length of time or number of performances for a production.

run-through: a rehearsal during which the entire show will be run in performance order.

sandbag: a bag of sand used to counterweight a rigged line or to add ballast to a unit.

scale: in drafting; the relative measured scale the drafting represents.

scene shift: a moment in which technicians change the locations of design elements during a performance.

script: the text of a play.

secondary colors: colors that can be created by mixing two neighboring primary colors together.

selective focus: in lighting; one of the four functions of light, the use of contrast to guide the eyes of the audience to the action.

set: the scenic environment designed for a play.

set dressing: items on the set that the performers do not handle, but add atmosphere and detail.

set props: large prop items and furniture pieces.

sheet goods: building materials such as plywood sold in flat sheets, typically measuring 4 feet by 8 feet.

shift light: a lighting state used during scene changes to facilitate the work and indicate to the audience that these moments are not part of the action of the play.

show curtain: a specialty curtain designed as scenery for a play.

shutters: in lighting; the metal flags that allow the beam to be shaped in the fixture.

signal chain: in sound; the path through the system the electronic signal is routed. Aka signal path.

signal to noise ratio: in sound; the balance of desired electronic signal to unwanted electric interference leaking into the signal.

signal path: see "signal chain."

site-specific theatre: theatre performed in a nontraditional location.

sitzprobe: a rehearsal for singers and the orchestra in which the singers are seated or at least not following their set blocking.

skin: in scenery; the top surface of a scenic unit.

sky drop: a large drop representing the sky on a stage.

slip stage: a stage wagon, often large enough to hold an entire setting.

smoke machine: an effects unit that produces a vapor for fog and smoke.

snow cradle: a sling used to drop dry materials like snow and confetti from above a stage.

soft-cover flat: a temporary wall usually built with a wood frame, the face of the frame being covered in a fabric.

soft-edged light: in lighting; an instrument whose beam fades toward its edge, causing the perimeter to be indistinguishable.

sound system: the system of equipment allowing for controlled playback for a production.

source device: in sound; any input device bringing a signal into a sound system.

spacing rehearsal: a rehearsal conducted once scenery has been loaded into a theatre so the cast can make the adjustment from the tapelines of the rehearsal room to the physical setting.

special effect: any unusual effect used for a performance, these may be physical, pyrotechnic, auditory, or based in light.

spot/spotting down: in lighting; the narrowing of an instruments beam.

stage crew: the group of technicians needed for performance of a play.

stage combat: movement created to create the illusion of combat while keeping the performers safe.

stage direction: a system of directions given from the actor's perspective to describe areas of the stage.

stage house: the stage area between the proscenium and the upstage wall including the stage, wings, grid, and fly system.

stage monitor: a system that allows actors backstage to hear the dialogue being spoken on stage.

stock scenery: scenic elements built and stored for reuse by the theatre.

stock size: a predetermined size that stock elements are built in for easy reuse.

straight-run platform wagon: a platform equipped with fixed casters to run in a straight direction on stage.

strip light: a multi-cell lighting fixture typically used to light drops. Aka border light.

stumble-through: an early rehearsal held after show blocking is complete to show designers the shape and flow if the show.

subtractive color: in lighting; the use of filters to limit the spectrum of light.

sugar-glass: a term used to describe breakaway prop items that appear as glass to the audience. Though sugar can be used, resins are frequently employed to manufacture these breakaway items.

swatch: a small piece of fabric that accompanies designs for color and textural reference.

swivel caster: a caster with a rotating base allowing for it to roll at any given angle.

teaser: traditionally the first short and wide drape upstage of the proscenium. This drape masks the first electric.

technical notes: rehearsal and performance refinements or correctives regarding the technical elements of a production.

technical rehearsals: rehearsals that focus on refining the technical elements of a production.

template: in lighting; a cut-out placed in a lighting instrument to project an image. Aka gobo.

tertiary colors: colors mixed from a primary and its neighboring secondary color.

thumbnail sketch: an early, rough sketch of a design idea.

tie-off cleat: a piece of stage hardware used to secure a line for quick adjustment.

title block: a window of text on a scaled drafting that lists the subject of the draft, its scale, and other pertinent information.

thrust theatre: a theatre space where the audience surrounds three sides of the playing area.

top of show: the beginning of a play or performance.

tormentor: The first set of tall and narrow drapes hung upstage of the proscenium and used to mask the wings of a stage.

transmission: in lighting; the percentage of source light allowed to pass through a color filter.

trap: an opening in the floor of a stage or platform used to facilitate appearances and disappearances.

transducer: a device that translates an electronic sound waveform into a physical sound wave or reverses the process.

twist-lock connector: in lighting; a three-blade connector in a circular formation equipped with a locking ground.

unbalanced cable: in sound; a cable equipped with only two wires that has little resistance to electric interference.

valence: a horizontal curtain designed to mask the rod or batten.

vehicle: one of the components of paint. The vehicle allows the paint to be spread and either evaporates, cures, or is absorbed.

wagon: a rolling platform.

washes: in scenic painting; translucent paints used to layer colors on scenery.

wet tech: a technical rehearsal incorporating cast and crew.

wing: the area outside the playing area of a stage that is unseen by the audience.

wood grain: in lumber; the longitudinal arrangement of wood fibers. In painting; a finish imitating the surface of wood.

yoke: in lighting; the U-shaped support connecting the lighting instrument and the C-clamp allowing for a tilting action.

CPSIA information can be obtained
at www.ICGtesting.com
Printed in the USA
LVHW062043110721
692146LV00001B/5

9 781945 398872